HELLENISM AND HINDUISM

HELLENISM AND HINDUISM

D.N. TRIPATHI

INDIAN INSTITUTE OF ADVANCED STUDY
RASHTRAPATI NIVAS, SHIMLA

First published 2004

ISBN 81-7986-044-2

Published by
The Secretary
Indian Institute of Advanced Study
Rashtrapati Nivas, Shimla-171005

Typeset at Sai Graphic Design, New Delhi
and printed at Pearl Offset Pvt. Ltd., Kirti Nagar, New Delhi

In memory
of
my mother

Contents

Preface

The following pages embody the results of my work at the Indian Institute of Advanced Study, where I was appointed a fellow on 14 May 1999. The concepts discussed in this book are some of the Great Ideas of the Greek and Indian cultures. These concepts are the Perennial Philosophy of the civilized world. It is the "Indianness" and the "Helleneness" of the two great civilizations which were responsible for the growth of the basic tenets of the Oriental and Occidental civilizations, respectively. In undertaking the study I had no desire of propounding any theory or building any model; my sole intention was to examine and present systematically, in a concise form, the basic facets of the two great cultures on the basis of the latest archaeological researches and analyses of texts, from the earliest period to the classical phase which was an age of innovations and was therefore remarkable and fascinating in many respects.

The source material for this study is abundant and is available in many languages and archaeological artifacts of the Indo-European world. This stands in the way of a full evaluation of the different aspects of these cultures as I do not know many of the languages (except Greek, Sanskrit, and English) and have not examined the archaeological data kept in various museums of European countries. I had some opportunity to study the Greek material kept in different museums there. But, that was long back in 1971-76. I do not know how much more archaeological material must have come into light. However, I have tried to update my knowledge through journals and books published thereafter. I am fully conscious of the numerous defects that this study suffers from. No one else but I am responsible for this.

I record my thanks to the Governing Body of the Institute

and its Directors, Professor Mrinal Miri, (for the letter of invitation to join as a Fellow), Professor S. C. Bhattacharya (now a National Fellow at the Institute), and Professor V. C. Srivastava for the facilities that were offered to me. I offer my regards and thanks to Professor Ramashray Roy, an eminent political thinker, for having gone into the manuscript minutely and correcting it.

Gratefulness cannot be expressed in words to the Philosopher-Historian, Professor Govinda Chandra Pande, Chairman of the Governing Body of this Institute and my *gurudeva* but for whose guidance and help it would never have been possible to complete this project. I am also grateful to my wife, Smt. Leela Tripathi, who, despite her ill health, kept company and encouraged me for this work by taking over all the responsibilities at home.

Shimla D.N. Tripathi
25 October 2003

CHAPTER 1

Introduction

Hellenism and Hinduism: An Archaeological and Historical Study

Hellenism and Hinduism are basically responsible for the growth of the basic tenets of the Occidental and Oriental cultures, respectively. Yet, both the religions are not properly understood because their nature and the basic forms have not been properly understood or analyzed. Since Hellenism and Hinduism represent the real spirit and values of the two different world-views of the Indo-European people living in two extremes of the geographical horizons of the Indo-European world, and that they have a long tradition and history much of which still survive in their cultures, it has been decided to investigate the origins and development of these two great traditions in order to see why the spirit of Hellenism is lost in the country of its birth whereas the spirit of Hinduism still exists in India.

The purpose of the present study is to analyze the circumstances for the origin and growth of both the religions in their respective geographical areas on the basis of archaeological and historical studies done in this area during the last fifty years.

The term Hellenism is derived from the ancient Greek word '*Hellinsmos*' meaning "to speak or act Greek". Though the meaning of this term is fairly well established by common usage, it is in itself ambiguous. In very late Greek literature, with special reference to the Jews (e.g. the Septuagint and the Book of Maccaliees) it implies the adoption not only of the Greek language but also of Greek manners. Elsewhere it denotes the ancient Greek culture in all its phases; for long before the 4th century BC it is possible to detect Greek influence in many parts of the world from Spain to Southern Russia, from Gaul to the Carthagian territories of North Africa. However, the term Hellenism, as applied by the German historian Droysen, has come to be used most commonly of the later stages of Greek culture, from the date of Alexander's conquest to the final passing away of those who were influenced by Greek culture though non-Greek by birth, had adopted the Greek language and way of life. The principal center of such influence was the city of Alexandria, which affected the whole of the known world from western Europe to India. Thus the term Hellenism broadly refers to the fusion of Greek culture with the older cultures of Asia Minor, Syria, Mesopotamia, and Egypt during the three centuries after the death of Alexander the Great in 323 BC. From this cultural fusion developed the idea of the *ecumene* (inhabited world) belonging to all civilized men. A man was a Hellene if he spoke Greek and shared Greek custom and law, regardless of where he lived. A new dialect, *Koine* (common Greek), became universal. Ultimately, this fusion led to the composite cultures of the Roman Empire in the East.

Hans Jonas (1963, p. 10) has distinguished four historical phases of Greek culture: (1) before Alexander, the classical phase as a national culture; (2) after Alexander, Hellenism as a cosmopolitan secular culture; (3) later Hellenism as a pagan religious culture; and (4) Byzantinism as a Greek Christian culture. The transition from the first to the second phase is for the most part explained as an autonomous Greek development. In the second phase (300 BC- first century AD) the Greek spirit was represented by the great rival schools of philosophy, the Academy, the Epicureans, and above all the Stoics, while at the same time the Greek-oriental synthesis was progressing. The transition from the third phase, the turning to religion of ancient civilizations as a whole and of the Greek mind with it, was the work of profoundly un-Greek forces which, originating in the East, entered history as new factors. Between the rule of Hellenistic secular and the final defensive position of the late Hellenism turned religious lie three centuries of revolutionary spiritual movements which effected this transformation, among which the gnostic movement occupies a prominent place.

For the purpose of present study Hellenism is defined as a body of humanistic and classical ideals (also described as "Classical Humanism") associated with ancient Greece (specifically developed by the Greek cities in the 5th and 4th centuries BC) including reason, the pursuit of knowledge and arts, moderation, civic responsibility, and bodily development (a revival of Hellenism fostered by some British Victorians). I have considered only the first phase of the Greek culture of Hans Jonas. Matthew Arnold (1875) has correctly applied it to that form of culture, or ideal of life, of which ancient Greek is taken as a type. He considers that the great movement of Renaissance was an uprising and reinstatement of man's intellectual impulses and Hellenism.

It is more than a century ago that the speculations and astonishing discoveries of Heinrich Schliemann opened the way for archaeological research into the prehistoric period of Greek civilization. Today, on the basis of both direct and indirect evidences, we are in a position to form an image of the remotest past of Greek world—a world that once belonged to the sphere of mythology. Researches and excavations carried out throughout the area extending from Thrace and Macedonia to Cyprus and Crete have produced a prodigious quantity of objects dated to the Stone and Bronze Ages. The limits that once circumscribed Greek prehistory have thus been enormously extended and, crossing the threshold of our age, it is now possible to enter the vanished world of Pleistocene. Light has been cast on ages formerly obscure, on unknown periods and phases of time, and the true depths of the prehistory of the country have been revealed.

It is generally accepted that every civilization, even such a brilliant one as that of the classical era in Greece, must first be regarded as the outcome of the tradition. The study of this tradition, without preconceived limits, is therefore imperative. As Blegen (1928), one of the most distinguished scholars in the field of prehistoric Greece, has pointed out, the "Greek-ness" of the Myceneans is not without consequence. "The definite recognition of the Myceneans as Greeks", he says, "calls for something more than mere passing mention. Let it be an early stage in the history of that race, perhaps before Hellenic speech had yet been fully evolved. Nonetheless it demonstrates the inherent strength of the Greek people and their astonishing power of survival; they still exist and flourish today, retaining their distinctive character, their language, and their exclusiveness along with their cohesiveness, despite intense individualism. Apart possibly from the Chinese, there are few, if any, other comparable peoples in their tenacity to endure. In their long history they have at least three times blossomed out into world leadership in culture: in the Late Mycenaean Age, in the Classical period, and in the heyday of the Byzantine Empire". Blegen probably did not know the tenacity of the Indian culture?

The decisive argument in favor of this view was the great achievement of Michel Ventris's decipherment of the Linear B script. There can be little doubt now that the tablets written in the Greek language have become almost historical documents thanks to his efforts. They offer a definitive basis for the identification of the Hellenic character of the Mycenean civilization. The exceptional duration and continuity of the tradition of Greek civilization means we have to go back in time as far as possible in order to discern its roots.

There were two "Golden Ages" in Bronze Age Greece: The New Palace Period on the Minoan Crete and the culminating phase of the Mycenean period on the Mainland. The Minoan civilization, eastern in character though not in spirit, was not only the finest achievement of the Aegean Bronze Age, but also the first advanced civilization to flourish on the European soil. From its remote position in the extreme southwest corner of the continent, the Minoan civilization shone out brilliantly over both the Aegean and the Mainland. Before its own light dimmed, it succeeded in illuminating the path ahead which the more primitive peoples of Helladic Greece could follow, and in providing, through its own achievements, the spark of inspiration they needed to create their own new civilization, the Mycenean.

The Mycenean civilization did in fact continue along the path paved by its predecessors up to the end of the Bronze Age, but it had a vigor and spirit of its own and a more decisive influence on later Greek history, since its own character determined to a large extent the character of Greek civilization in the subsequent Archaic Period, a period reflected in the epics of Homer.

The disintegration of the Mycenean state did not bring about the end of the Mycenean civilization. Nor did the eventual destruction of this civilization wipe out all its achievements. To some degree at least, the Creto-Mycenean heritage survived and was handed down through subsequent generations. This happened at a critical turning point in history: the transition between the Bronze Age and the Iron Age. The change in culture took place at approximately the same period throughout the whole of the Eastern Mediterranean. The changes, which came about during this period in the whole of the surrounding areas had important results in Greece, now emerging from the obscure period, called the Greek "Middle Ages". The term is misleading, but it does reflect our present ignorance of this new critical phase. Most of the recent researches seek to match the information given in the epic poems with the archaeological evidence. We can certainly form an idea and speculate about its character and trace the path of the Creto-Mycenean heritage in the Classical Hellenic Civilization. It is now a well-established fact that in spite of all the upheavals of the "Dark Ages"; there was no break between the Mycenean and post-Mycenean world. What exactly was the heritage and how was it handed down? How extensive was it and how significant from a historical point of view? The answer to these questions could be found in the study of the Mycenean and post-Mycenean civilizations and in the study of the ethnic and linguistic groups in prehistoric Greece.

There is plenty of evidence, gathered both recently and in the past, to show that elements of the Mycenean civilization either survived into or reappeared in historical times; the idea of the city-state, the megaron-shaped plan of the Greek temple, the nuclei of the epics, the language of the Greeks. For all the excellent work being done in this broad field of research, the subject has not by any means been exhausted. Indeed, new fields of study have opened up especially after the decipherment of the Mycenean script. Leaving on one side all other manifestations of culture, we may observe that the ethical value of the Mycenean alone played a decisive role in shaping the culture of historical Greece.

The heritage from the heroic age influenced not only the cults and myths but also the entire spiritual life and education of the Greeks in historical times. The idea of national unity had its roots in the heroic age, and again it was in this period that the Greeks turned whatever a treaty or alliance needed to be justified historically. It was the common tradition more than a common language or country, which united the Greek race. The survival and transmitting of this tradition would naturally have been impossible had there been no ethnic continuity in Greece. The Mycenean at the end of the Mycenean period—the people who had handed down this tradition—were basically an Indo-European people. But they were also Greek. It was precisely this mixing of tribes and cultures, which has produced the Mycenean "miracle". Also, there are no doubts that some fairly substantial remnants of the Mycenean population remained. They were subdued or transferred where they could do no harm. Some were sent to distant coasts or islands, such as Cyprus, where there is no doubt that they had an influence on later developments. This is shown by the fact that the greatest cultural progress in historical times was achieved in Attica—a region not settled by the newly arrived Greeks.

It is a truism that the creative spirit of Crete inspired the Helladic world. And we can appreciate how much poor the Mycenean civilization would have been without the influence of the Minoan by noting the much lower level of civilization achieved by other European countries in the Bronze Age.

The old belief that there was a gulf between the prehistoric and historical times supported by the theory that the "northerner" tribe descended into Greece in c. 1100 BC bringing the Olympian gods and the Greek spirit to the "pre-Hellenic world" has now been abandoned, for Greek history no longer begins with the coming of the Dorians. The new age, which begins at the dawn of historical times, is not completely cut off from the past. More and more evidence of Mycenean influence is coming to light all the time. And it is certain that the ethnic continuity of the Greeks from the beginning of the second millennium BC will be established, whether or not the present interpretation of the Mycenean texts continue to be accepted.

We know that the Myceneans are part of the Hellenic World and tradition; consequently, the heritage they bequeathed to later generations must have played an important role in forming the civilizations of both Archaic and Classical Greece.

Thus far is the story of continuing traditions and culture of the Greek people. The same story is seen repeated in the history of Hinduism in India. Hinduism is the title applied to that form of a religion, which prevails among the vast majority of the present population in India. Brahmanism, which is the term generally used to designate the higher and more philosophical form of modern Hinduism, is more properly restricted to that development of the faith which, under the Brahman influence, succeeded to Vedism, or the animistic worship of the greater powers of Nature. The term Hindu is entirely a linguistic one, which denotes the people who were living beyond the eastern side of the river Sindhu. Hinduism did not give this name to Hindus. The foreign writers and travelers gave it to the people living in India or Hindustan. A common term for the ancient Aryan settlements in the Punjab was 'the Seven Rivers' (*sapta-sindhavah*). The name 'Hindu' appears in the form of 'Hindus' in the inscription on the monument of Darius Hystaspes near Persepolis in c. 486 BC; 'Hod(d)u' in the later Hebrew literature and in the modern form in Herodotus (c. 440 BC). It seems that due to phonetic change the term Sindhu changed into Hindu and the foreign travellers and writers designated the land beyond the 'Sindhu' or Indus as the land of Hindus or Hindustan in later times. No where do we find this appellation for India in the ancient literary tradition of India. The term always referred to the people, whether Muslims, Christians, Parsees or any other races, who came and lived in India. These people evolved a view of life, a social structure, economic institutions, political system, the morality, the religion and philosophy, the art and literature, the science and commerce etc., in a long process of experiences since the Rigvedic period until now. This value and view of life is known as Hinduism.

Thus Hinduism is not a form but a concept. It is not a religion but a life behavior. It is not a communal sect for Hinduism does not have a single Prophet, single God, single book, single philosophy and faith but the people who lived in a geographical, political, and cultural boundary known as Hindustan or India. Hinduism includes people of all religious faiths—Buddhism, Jainism, Vaishnavism, Shaivism, Sikhism, Parsism, Islam, and Christianity—who live in India and follow their religious principles and worship their God without any restrictions. Hinduism accepts them all who believe in Vedas or abuses the Vedas in their philosophical or religious doctrines.

In short, Hinduism is the realization of values, in theory and practice. Religion is the realization of only the ethical values preter-social and social. In preter-social is included the superhuman and subhuman whereas in social there is a correlational human and gregational human. Hinduism is a value-loaded predicate. Value is one word for 'subject's attitude to object'. Attitude in its turn is analyzed as 'disposition to regulate the responses to'. The term 'value' therefore means subject's disposition to regulate the response to objects. As such values are subject-object relations.

The subject of Hinduism, in many of its varied phases, has been studied by different foreign and Indian scholars. The purpose of this study is to discuss, in a general way, the progressive evolution of Hinduism from the Vedic religion up to the rise of Puranic Brahmanism, and to group the facts, as far as possible, in their historical setting. Such a study has been done on the basis of the Vedic and Puranic literature, although some of the scholars may disagree with the authenticity of the two sources as they might believe that 'the Vedas simply embody the naïve speculations of the early Indo-Aryans on the character and functions of their gods', whereas the writings of the 'later Brahman period were compiled by the priestly class to support its claim to the leadership of the Aryan community'. Brahmanical Hinduism dates from the most ancient period. The orderly progress of the religious development was never interrupted although many foreign invasions took place in the centuries following the birth of Buddha and Mahavira. It is true that the foreigners as well as non-Vedic religions (Buddhism and Jainism) profoundly influenced the course of Hinduism, both the religious and social life of the Hindu; however, it is equally true that the basic form of Hinduism remained unaltered. The Vedic religion will be studied on the basis of the myths and religion as gleaned through the Vedic hymns. The foreign influences on the Vedic religion, as mentioned by some of the foreign scholars on the basis of coincidence between the Babylonian and early Hindu culture (the resemblance of Babylonian charms against diseases, evil spirits, and other invocations to those of the Atharva Veda) are not visible anywhere in Hinduism. If at all there was any Babylonian influence on Hinduism it was of a very late date and has been so thoroughly assimilated that it is no longer visible. The Greek campaigns of Alexander the Great produced little effect upon the history, politics, or religion of India.

The nature of Vedic gods and their transition from Vedism to Brahmanism and its contribution to the growth of Hinduism will be discussed. The chief contribution of this period seems to be: (a) a great system of religious philosophy known as Vedanta; (b) the supremacy of the *Brahman*; (c) the dogma of the efficacy of sacrifice; and (d) the doctrine of metaphysics. The anti-Brahmanical reaction in the sixth century BC and the rise of Buddhism and Jainism and its decline and the continuity of Brahmanism and the rise of Hinduism as depicted in the Puranas will be discussed. The Brahmanism, even during the ascendancy of Buddhism, never suffered complete extinction, though it undoubtedly lost much of its dignity and importance when Buddhism in North India and Jainism in south and western India enjoyed the patronage of ruling powers and were elevated to the rank of state religions. It is during the period of Purāṇas and epics that the reaction against Buddhism and Jainism was completed, and Hinduism, as we find in its existence now was firmly established. They accepted the tradition and adopted the religious myths, deities, and cults derived from races beyond the Brahmanical pale. For the purpose of this study Hinduism may be defined as "the collection of rites, beliefs, traditions, and mythologies that are sanctioned by the sacred books and ordinances of the ancient seers and a 'Hindu' as a man who follows the rules of conduct and ceremonial rites thus laid down for him."

The scope of this study is limited from the origins of the Hellenism and Hinduism to their growth and development up to the classical phases. As far as Hellenism is concerned the study of Minoan-Mycenean civilizations and the Iron Age culture of the Archaic period or the Homeric Age will be discussed and the traces of Classical Hellenism will be discerned. In India, the Indus and the Vedic cultures will be discussed on the basis of the archaeological remains and the Vedic texts. The traces of Hinduism in these periods will be discerned on the basis of critical analysis of the data thus available. The rise of non-vedic religions, the absorption of foreign elements in its fold and the final making of the form and shape of Hinduism in the Epic and Puranic period will thereafter be discussed.

Scholars differ vehemently on the question of the influence of Hellenism on Hinduism or *vice versa*. However, it is true that the evolution of philosophy, religion, and mythology has gone along parallel but independent paths. The grand poetry of the Vedas, the Epics, and Dramas of the succeeding epochs, the religious and philosophical speculations, the learned grammatical analysis of Panini and Patanjali, Mathematics, all the rich, brilliant and intellectual achievements of ancient Indians, though akin to the Greeks in many ways, but are more richly endowed. All these studies were developed much before the Hellenic culture came into existence. The question does not interest itself solely the Indianist and the Hellenist, but all those who are interested in tracing the evolution of the antecedents of their modern culture and civilization, the different phases of their national culture and progress. It is a curious fact that few races have disappeared so utterly in India as the Greeks.

Each Greek divinity was regarded as the founder of his or her own cult; Juno at Argos; Apollo at Delphi and Delos; Neptune and Pallas at Athene, and so forth. In the eyes of the Persians the Greeks were barbarians and odious idolaters. They carried on fierce wars against the ungodly, upsetting their idols and burning their temples wherever the politics of Darius and the passion of Xerxes led them. At present we know for certain that most of it, if not all worships of ancient Greece, originated in Asia. There are many things in common between the religions of the Persians, Indians, and Greeks which indicate a common origin of these religious systems. As far as the origin of Parsism and Brahmanism is concerned it is manifestly clear that they have a common origin.

Greece also notwithstanding the extent of her pagan period and the subsequent vehemence of her Christian creed, still cherishes in popular rhymes, the legends which are unmistakably pre-Hellenic, and which from all appearance relate to the first Aryan migration from Asia. Such, for example, is the legend of Charos whose name so often appears in popular Greek lore. This Charos is the god of death, almost all his attributes recall those of *Kala* of the Indians. At any rate, we are now certain that this diffusion of the religious ideas took place at some remote time and that all those ancient worships pertained, like those of Greece, Italy, Persia, and India to one system or rather to one primordial unity.

The origin of the Greek religion should be ultimately traced to India. The myth of Zeus, his contest with Prometheus, and his human passions and attributes point to Indian sources, particularly to *Indra* in the Vedas. The name Kronos may have been derived from the Sanskrit word *krano* (creating for himself) and has nothing to do with Chronos "time". Megasthenese tells us a good deal about the Hindu representative of Dionysius to whom Arrian calls Siva Dionysius. The character of the Prometheus-myth has been conclusively proved to be of Indo-European character by Kuhn (Banerjee, 1995, p. 277). If the name Athena really corresponds to the Sanskrit *Ahana*, the dawning and Athenaia to *ahania* "the day bright", as Max Müller supposes, we may also regard her as Indo-European goddess. Hermes, the messenger and the right hand of Zeus, is identical with *Sarameyos*, the names of the two dogs of *Yama*, the mythic watchdogs in the Veda. The Hindu gods and goddesses may have certain similarities with the Greek gods and goddesses which seem to come out of the common Indo-European origin of both the cultures. Moreover, the Hindu theory of the idol is in sharp contrast with that of the Greeks. To the former human form is merely the ephemeral clothing of the soul, in which, unhappily, it is forced to linger for a time. The worship that substituted idols for ideal-forms has to be traced back to the end of the Vedic period. It is not however a mark of early Brahmanism, nor is it a pronounced feature of the age of Buddha.

The Logos doctrine of the Greeks seems to have been imported from India. In the Brahmanic period, the Rigvedic *vac*, speech, becomes more and more like the Greek Logos and in this period it may truthfully be said, that "Word was God". In Greece, on the other hand, the conception of Logos begins with Heracleitus, and then passes on to the Stoics; is adopted by Philo; becomes a prominent feature of neo-Platonism; and reappears in the Gospel of St. John. It is legitimate to infer that Heracleitus might have received the idea indirectly from the contemporary Indian philosophers. There is also similarity between the other forms of early Greek and Hindu philosophy. "Both Thales and Parmenides were anticipated by Hindu sages and the Eleatic school seems to be but reflexion of the Upanishads. The doctrines of Anaximander and Heracleitus are not known first in Greece and they are evidently borrowed from India. Before the sixth century BC, all the religious-philosophical ideas of Pythagoras were current in India" (vide L.von Schroeder, Pythagoras, quoted in Banerjee, 1995, p. 281). Thus it is clear that the blending of the two peoples, indigenous and Indo-Europeans, gave birth to Hellenism. The Indo-Europeans entered Greece with certain personal already evolved deities. We find that anthropomorphism was the strongest bias of the Hellenes' religious imagination which was effaced by the forms of faith and speculation from the East.

As against the Greek religion, which has many things in common with the Hindu religion, the Greek philosophy differs to some extent from the Hindu philosophy. The Greeks had no sacred books, like the Vedas, which dictated to them any views concerning the origin of the world or the constitution of Nature, and which they would have considered immoral to disbelieve. In fact, when Heracleitus boldly declared that 'neither God nor man made the Kosmos', there was no authoritative Greek myth or theologic dogma to gainsay him (Banerjee, 1995, p. 286). Of the great philosophers of the sixth century, Pythagoras, Empedokles, Xenophanes, and Heracleitus, were also directly concerned with the philosophy of religion, with speculations on the Nature, and the true definition of the godhead. But the main trend of their speculations ran counter to the anthropomorphic theory of divinity; and they tend to define God not as a person, but rather as the highest spiritual metaphysical, or even physical power or function of the universe; and there is a common tendency in the sixth century philosophy to depart from the theistic to pantheistic.

It is a highly suggestive fact however, that the dawn of the scientific speculation in Greece should coincide with a great religious movement in India when the doctrines of Buddha gathered up the scattered beliefs of Brahmanic polytheism into one energetic synthesis of Buddhism. The monotheistic tendency is visible in Greece as elsewhere, and the gods gradually lose their independent autocratic position under Zeus, who in later systems is identified as intelligence and Goodness. I have tried to examine the Greek and Hindu views on the origin of cosmos and its relationship with man—the two fundamental aspects of any religion or philosophy.

The subject that I have chosen to discuss "Hellenism and Hinduism" has a very wide spectrum. Much has been written on this subject. What I have done here is not to repeat all that has been said to date. The basic nature and the temper of any civilization can be judged through their language and religious speculations. Scholars have been working with a bias that both the Greeks and the Hindus came in their respective countries from outside and implanted their culture in those countries. We find a lot of things in common between these two great civilizations. This definitely indicates that the ideas and the language that both of them share between themselves must have come into existence due to close contacts. The differences are simply apparent and can be attributed to the local, ecological, and environmental differences and the time depth that must have elapsed in between.

The area and topics of discussion on this subject could be quite wide. Since many scholars, both in India and outside, have discussed some of the topics at length, I have selected some basic concepts from the two cultures to discuss in this monograph. The nature, origin, and evolution of languages, the concept of man and the idea of humanism, the concept of cosmology and cosmogony, the nature of justice, social justice, and the meaning and nature of ethics would be my main concern, as these elements form the very core of any culture and civilization. At the end, a short overview of the conclusions arrived at in the above area will be summarized for the sake of those who would like to have a simple overview of the subject.

CHAPTER 2

Origin and Evolution of Indo-European Languages

THE ORIGIN OF LANGUAGE

Man is often defined by the archaeologists as *homo technicos* because they find only material remains to identify him. It would rather be correct to define man as *homo vocalis*. Since we the archaeologists cannot find any tangible evidence of the language before the fourth millennium BC (although being fully aware of the fact that it must have originated much earlier!), we define him simply as a 'tool-maker'. What therefore I propose in this chapter is to discuss some of the widely respected and repeated theories about the origin of the languages in general and that of Indo-European (IE) languages in particular, with which the origin and evolution of the Greek and Indian civilizations are linked with. Most of these theories are based on the presumption that Indo-European languages must have originated somewhere other than India or Greece from where we get the best and most ancient literature in this language. Thereafter, I will argue the insufficiency of these theories which ignore some of the important counter-evidences available in them.

The striking parallels between biology and linguistics, particularly in their evolutionary aspect, have been generally recognized since at least the mid-nineteenth century. In one of his few references to language, Charles Darwin pointed out in 1871 that "the formation of different languages and of distinct species, and the proofs that both have been developed through a gradual process, are curiously parallel". But, for biologists the monogenetic origin of *Homo sapiens* is now generally accepted (though supporters of "Multiregional Evolution" would dispute this point), and, for them, the notion that the Indo-European peoples have no known biological relatives would be ludicrous. Yet, for most linguists, a common origin of all human languages is very much in doubt, and the belief that Indo-European has no known linguistic relatives is not only a safe position, but also practically a merit badge for sober scholarship. To be sure, the monogenetic origin of *Homo sapiens* need not *necessarily* entail the monogenesis of human languages; the two topics are, and should be kept, distinct, and when we find correlation between biology and linguistics, we insist that these correlations be arrived at independently. If the splendid genetic isolation of Indo-European can be maintained, the question of monogenesis becomes moot. The American linguist William Dwight Whitney (1967:383), said: "Linguistic science is not, now, and cannot, ever hope to be, in condition to give an authoritative opinion respecting the unity or variety of our species".

Despite the pessimistic attitude of Whitney and other European scholars, some scholars have sought to find evidence of more comprehensive classification of the world's languages. In several works published during the first quarter of the twentieth century, the Italian linguist Alfredo Trombetti sought to establish the monogenesis of human languages by comparing lexical and grammatical roots from languages and language families around the world. As early as 1905 he presented a strong *prima facie* case for the monogenesis of human languages. In the New World, from roughly 1910–1930, the American linguist, Edward Sapir, and his student Morris Swadesh, made a number of sweeping proposals for the consolidation of numerous native American language families and its genetic affinity with Sino-Tibetan. Swadesh was interested in establishing a worldwide network of linguistic relationships. During the early 1960s two Russian scholars, Vladislav Illich-Svitych and Aron Dolgopolsky, revived an earlier proposal of the Dane, Holger Pedersen, which grouped Indo-European with several other families of Eurasia and North Africa in a Nostratic phylum. In classical Nostratic theory, Indo-European is one of the six related subgroups, the others being Afro-Asiatic, Kartvelian, Uralic, Altaic, and Dravidian. The

American linguist Joseph Greenberg has probably made greatest contributions to taxonomy.

Despite the path-breaking work of these scholars, the majority of the linguistic community still adheres to the belief that Indo-European has no known linguistic relatives, and none is ever likely to be demonstrated, because—so the argument goes—beyond the time depth of Indo-European all traces of genetic affiliation have been obliterated by ceaseless phonetic and semantic erosion. But Ruhlen (1999, p. 272) feels that such a conclusion would be incorrect. Also, the proposition that the monogenesis of language cannot be demonstrated on the basis of linguistic evidence is equally incorrect. He says:

Belief in these erroneous assertions is based largely on extra-linguistic criteria and *a priori* assumptions, rather than on a serious survey of the world's linguistic literature . . . *all the world's languages do share a common origin* (emphasis mine).

Ruhlen is aware of the implications of the theory of monogenesis of languages. He is of the opinion that 'the search for linguistic "relationships" is now over (or should be), since it no longer makes sense to ask if two languages (or two language families) are related. *Everything* is related, and the question to be investigated within or among different families is the *degree* of their relationships, not the fact of it'. He further argues that use of typological traits in genetic classification is more controversial, the generally accepted view being that such traits are in fact not indicative of genetic relationships. The preliminary data, he says, 'indicate that there is greater genetic component in typology than has previously been assumed' (p. 273).

The second consequence of monogenesis is that it becomes possible, at least theoretically, to compare a phylogenetic tree of the human family based on linguistic traits with one based on biological traits. Cavalli-Sforza et al. (1988) are of the view that the correlation between biological and linguistic classifications is most intimate: "Linguistic families correspond to group of populations with very few, easily understood overlaps, and their origin can be given a time frame. Linguistic superfamilies show remarkable correspondence..., indicating parallelism between genetic and linguistic development". On the basis of these arguments, Ruhlen hopefully concludes that: 'perhaps when both biological and linguistic taxonomy have been elaborated more confidently and in greater detail, the many parallels and similarities between the two fields will come to be viewed not as "curious" but as natural' (p. 274).

The theory of monogenesis of languages is not acceptable to a majority of scholars working in the field of genetics or linguistic taxonomy. At present, Indo-European language family, with its various sub-families, is considered an important and one of the most ancient separate groups with no genetic relationship with one group or the other. It is the most widely distributed (both temporally and spatially) language and is still being studied as a separate family by a majority of the scholars.

THE PROBLEM OF INDO-EUROPEAN LANGUAGES

Although scholars always accepted the Vedas as the earlier literature available to humanity they could, however, not place them in exact chronological order. The antiquity and importance of Sanskrit language were first realized and accepted by the western scholars when Sir William Jones, an English Judge, serving in India at the High Court of Calcutta, in his "Third Anniversary Discourse" in 1786 to the Asiatic Society of Bengal said:

> The Sanskrit language, whatever may be its antiquity, is of wonderful structure; more perfect than the Greek and more copious than the Latin, and more exquisitely refined than either; yet bearing to both of them a stronger affinity, both in the roots of verbs and in the forms of grammar, than could have been produced by accident; so strong that no philologer could examine them all three without believing them to have sprung from some common source, which, perhaps no longer exists. There is a similar reason, though not quite so forcible, for supposing that both the Gothic and the Celtic, though blended with a different idiom, had the same origin with the Sanskrit; and the Old Persian might be added to the same family, if this were the place for discussing any question concerning the antiquity of Persia.

This brilliant observation has been further developed and analyzed by generations of scholars in many works and there is little doubt that Sir William Jones was right. The links, evident or not, between these languages concern a small part of their vocabulary and a large part of their grammar. Their common vocabulary includes mainly the numerals, the personal and some other pronouns, words which express degrees of kinship, names of animals and plants, and a few of the most common verbs. The grammatical relation between the languages emerges from both phonetics and inflexion, i.e., the manner of declining nouns, adjectives, derivations, etc., as well as from their syntax.

In 1813, the English scholar Thomas Young coined the term 'Indo-European' for this widely spread group of related languages. Sir William's is the first published recognition of the linguistic entity we now call "Proto-Indo-European" (or in German *Urindogermanische*). Since then investigators have sought, on the basis of the data provided by its several descendants, to reconstruct that "common source". Two hundred and some years after Sir William we know a great deal about Proto-Indo-European (PIE) though, in the absence of actual PIE records or, even better access to a native speaker or two, our knowledge will always be partial rather than complete. Our partial knowledge is of course subject to revision, both as new data become available (the discovery of Hittite and Tocharian at the beginning of this century has caused numerous revisions to our assumptions concerning Proto-Indo-European) and as our knowledge about language in general grows more sophisticated (advancing knowledge of linguistic typology particularly has suggested new ways of interpreting the possibilities of Proto-Indo-European).

But some very important questions regarding this clubbing together of the various languages under the 'Indo-European' arose:

(a) What is the historical reality underlying this relationship?
(b) Where did these languages come from?
(c) Did they derive from a single group of people who migrated?
(d) Or, is there an entirely different explanation?

This, in nutshell, is the Indo-European problem, and the enigma which has still not found a satisfactory answer. The protagonists of the theory of the Indo-European give us a simple explanation.

They suggest that the original language must have split up into dialects before the peoples who spoke it began to migrate in various directions. Eventually, the original language ceased to exist altogether. The external cause of its disappearance was the splitting up of the peoples into groups, who moved away from their original homeland and ceased to be in contact with one another. The internal cause was the gradual development of new idiomatic expressions in the language spoken by each separate group. Each group enriched its original vocabulary with words borrowed from other languages or words, which it made up itself and at the same time some of the words inherited from the original language, were forgotten. There were alterations in the phonological system: some old sounds vanished, others came to be pronounced differently, and some new sounds were created. Finally, similar changes came about in the declension of nouns and pronouns and the conjugation of verbs. It seems probable that the people who spoke the ancient Indo-European language did not belong to one race, rather can be regarded as having belonged to a group of tribes, some of which may have been of a common origin. This group must have split up into smaller ones, each with its own leaders, land, life, and migratory movement. As these smaller groups gradually moved further away from each other, they came to form new and separate people.

It is the central question for European and Asian Prehistory. If there were indeed major movements of early populations, which might have been responsible for this language distribution, then they should be reflected in the archaeological record, and they should be part of the story which the archaeologist tells. If on the other hand, folk movements are not the explanation, and the resemblance between the languages are the result of contacts between the various areas—perhaps through trade and exchange of marriage partners—then the archaeological record, properly interpreted, should also reflect this. There is very little in the early histories or literature of the languages concerned to explain the links between them. Hence, this is one of the most notable and enduring problems in the prehistory of the Old World.

The Indo-European languages begin to appear in the written record in the Bronze and Iron ages. The earliest attested languages are first encountered between Greece and northern India and consist of: Anatolian, the proper names of which are first attested in Akkadian trading documents of c.1900 BC; Indo-Aryan, which first emerges in northern Syria in the Mitanni kingdom by c. 1600–1500 BC; and Greek, which is known from the palace documents of the Myceneans, in the so-called Linear B scripts, from at least 1300 BC. By the Iron age (c. 100–1 BC) we have evidence for the Italic, Messapic, Celtic, and Germanic stocks in the west, the Balkan languages such as Thracian, Dacian and Illyrian, Phrygain in Anatolia, and first hand evidence of Iranian. The other IE languages, other than occasional parahistorical references, do not appear in written records until the first millennium AD or later. This distribution of the Indo-European languages of Eurasia allows us to see the full "historical" distribution of the Indo-European languages of Eurasia.

Czech linguist Hrozny (1931) read them in 1924 several issues concerning the Aryan problem seemed to have been solved. Ever since then authority of the Vedic literature for interpreting the Indo-European problem has been accepted by scholars. The early observations of Sir William Jones were soon followed by the much more systematic linguistic researches of scholars such as Friedrich von Schlegel (1849) and Franz Bopp (1816, 1839) so that within fifty years the foundations of comparative linguistics were securely laid. The studies made on the basis of linguistic paleontology became acceptable to scholars only after the excavations of Boghazkeui in the Cuneiform script were unearthed. The most influential exponent of this approach was V. Gordon Childe, whose first paper 'On the date and origin of MinyanWare' was published in 1915. He argued that this characteristic pottery of the Middle Helladic period (c. 1900 BC) might be recognized as the indicator of the arrival for the first time of Greek speaking people in Greece. Childe was a philologist by training, although he later turned to archaeology, and in 1925 produced his great synthesis of European Prehistory, *The Dawn of European Civilization*. He combined the two approaches in the following year (1926) in his book *The Aryans*, where he surveyed each of the four major contestants for the status of the original homeland. He reviewed in turn the archaeological arguments for Asia, Central Europe, North Europe, and South Russia, opting firmly for the last of these.

Around the middle of the nineteenth century the whole study of the subject entered a new phase, which was again linguistic rather than archaeological, but linguistic in a different way—a single ancestral language for all the ancient languages, Sanskrit, Greek, Gothic, German etc.—the *Ursprache*, as the German scholars termed it (i.e., early or original homeland), which is now termed as Proto-Indo-European. The hypothetical homeland, the *Urheimat*, was logically to be found out. This method was lucidly set out in 1859 by Adolphe Picket (1877). Using an analogy with the branch of natural history where early and now extinct life forms are studied he called this approach 'linguistic paleontology'. Archaeology did not play any role in solving the problem of Indo-Europeans until the turn of the century. In 1902 the first scholar who dealt with this question from an archaeological point of view was Gustav Kossina (1902) who in his article '*Die indoeuropaische Frage archaologische beantwortel*' ('the Indo-European question answered archaeologically') concluded that the expansion of a group of people, supposedly indicated by the characteristic pottery termed 'corded ware', and by other associated artifacts, indicated 'the wide dispersal of Indo-Europeans in Germany. He thus proposed a north German homeland for the Indo-Europeans. Kossina was effectively the first to equate prehistoric peoples (and hence language) with pottery types, and he founded thereby a school of thought which survives with some scholars even to this day.

Although Childe later repudiated the approach which he took in the *Aryans* he remained deeply preoccupied with the question of Indo-European origins. In a work written just after the war (1950), *Prehistoric Migrations in Europe,* he returned again to the problem, and deployed in doing so all his remarkable command of the archaeological evidence. This time he no longer advocated a homeland in the steppes of South Russia. He did not also rely upon physical anthropology, instead on linguistic paleontology, and favored an Anatolian origin, seeing the Indo-European languages reaching Central and North Europe as late as Bronze Age. This allows us to see the full "historical" distribution of the Indo-European languages of Eurasia.

In the years that followed there were several important syntheses based largely on archaeological evidence, among them those of Bosch-Gimpera (1960, 1961), Giacopo Devoto (1962) and Hugh Hencken (1955) are some important ones. The most influential recent archaeological treatment has undoubtedly been that of Marija Gimbutas (1963, 1970), of the University of California at Los Angeles, who since 1963 has published a series of papers in which she locates the Indo-European homeland in the steppes of South Russia, very much as Childe did earlier. She, of course, has much more archaeological material with which to work. She uses the term 'Kurgan Culture' (i.e., the Barrow Culture, referring to the prehistoric burial mounds used in the area) to designate the material assemblages of these Proto-Indo-European speakers.

Gimbutas, building upon the work of Childe and before him Schrader (1890), thus lays considerable stress upon the arguments from the linguistic paleontology—the 'common words' to which she refers. In the further development of her theory, great weight is placed on especially significant features—for instance the Kurgans (burial mounds) themselves, and the corded ware which, since the early paper by Kossina, had attracted the attention of archaeologists. She is the leading exponent of the direct archaeological approach today.

THE HISTORY OF THE ARCHAEOLOGICAL AND LINGUISTIC STUDIES OF THE INDO-EUROPEAN PROBLEM

Latest Controversy

Renfrew of Cambridge University has expressed serious doubts about the earlier approaches in his book *Archaeology and Language* (1987), and is of the view that there should be a fundamental re-examination of the very foundations of this theory because:

(a) It is doubtful to reconstruct a Proto-Indo-European language, drawing upon the cognate forms of the words in the various Indo-European languages that are known;

(b) nor does modern archaeology so readily accept that the appearance of a new pottery style over a wide area necessarily betoken the migration of a whole people or conquest by warrior nomads; and that
(c) the whole assumption that in speaking of early Indo-Europeans we are necessarily dealing with nomads certainly merits re-examination.

Now, this issue lead us to two fundamental questions:

(i) How are we to explain, in linguistic terms, the emergence of languages which are clearly related to each other, and which we can classify into language groups?
(ii) And in what historical circumstances do we expect to find one language replaced by another in a particular area?

Renfrew is of the view that in search of the homeland of the Indo-Europeans the scholars have put forward the *arguments based upon circularity* (emphasis mine). He quotes Paul Freidrich's (1970) *'Proto European trees'*, one of the most thorough treatments to date in the field of linguistic paleontology:

> This short study treats one small portion of the language and culture system of the speakers of Proto-Indo-European dialects, who are assumed to have been scattered in a broad land over the steppes, forests and foot-hills between the western Caspian and the Carpathian, during roughly the fourth millennium and the first centuries of the third millennium BC.

Renfrew thinks that such an assumption is highly questionable. It is perhaps reasonable that the historical linguistics should be based upon archaeology but that archaeological interpretation should simultaneously be based upon linguistic analysis gives serious cause for concern. Each discipline assumes that the other can offer conclusions based upon sound independent evidence, but in reality one begins where the other ends. They are both relying on each other to prop up their mutual thesis.

Renfrew suggests that the Indo-European languages originated with the beginning of agriculture. According to him the first evidence of regular agricultural activities is to be seen in Anatolia around the seventh–sixth millennium BC, therefore, the Indo-European languages too may have originated there.

In 1988 a renewed interest in linguistic taxonomy gained an added boost from an unexpected quarter, when biologists—especially L.L. Sforza and his colleagues—found that a classification of the human population based on genetics bore a striking resemblance to the linguistic classification advocated by Greenberg and the Nostraticists. The high degree of correlation between the linguistic and genetic evidence for the spread of humans in prehistory led archaeologists, in particular Colin Renfrew, to propose that perhaps the time had come for a concerted interdisciplinary approach to the problems of human prehistory, in which the findings of comparative linguistics, human genetics, and archaeology would be integrated into a single overall hypothesis concerning the origin and spread of modern humans from Africa to the rest of the world, over the last 100,0000 years. Renfrew called this endeavor the "Emerging Synthesis", and Ruhlen's (1994) book *On the Origin of Languages: Studies in Linguistic Taxonomy* is an attempt in the direction of a linguistic contribution to this collective enterprise.

Ever since Renfrew's book has been published a new controversy has arisen amongst archaeologists and Indo-European linguists. Crossland (1992), while reviewing the books of Gramkrelidze & Ivanov (1984), Krantz (1988), and Markey & Greppin (1990), under the title 'When specialists collide: archaeology and Indo-European linguistics', has ably highlighted these problems. He says:

> The Indo-European (IE) question has recently become an arena for new radical explanations. The general consensus from the 1930s until 1984 was that the events which dispersed the languages classified as Indo-Europeans, *clearly related genetically* (emphasis mine), from Ireland and Scandinavia to Sri Lanka and Sinkiang by the Christian era began with *westward migrations of peoples of the Western Asiatic steppes* (emphasis mine), those of the 'Kurgan' cultures; the immediate ancestors of the Pontic region, in the 4th and 3rd millennia BC. Since 1984 three studies have proposed that the region of origin of the IE language family, or 'homeland', for brevity, should be located in Anatolia, or just to the east of it; and that the differentiation of Proto-Indo-European (PIE) may have begun as early as the 7th millennium BC. Gramkrelidze & Ivanov put the homeland in a zone running from the Balkans through Anatolia to Northern Mesopotamia, with a preference for Armenia. Krantz

concludes, apparently independently of Renfrew (1987), that IE speech evolved in eastern Anatolia and was brought into Europe by the Neolithic immigrants who introduced agriculture there. *When Worlds collide* includes much valuable discussion of this recent work.

Basic to the proposition involved when comparative linguistics is used in the reconstruction of historical events is the idea, first formulated and stated toward the end of the 18th century, that if a group of languages show similarity of certain kinds they must have evolved from dialects of an earlier unitary language (Sebeok, 1964; I-18, 58–70). In the 19th century the distribution of the IE languages c. 500 BC seemed best explained as resulting from migrations. They could hardly have remained a continuum over so large a zone even until c. 1000 BC. Lack of archaeological evidence for movements out of a possible homeland and into historical locations of IE languages has recently caused some archaeologists to distrust the entire hypothesis of a prehistoric IE-speaking people. Since the 1960s most linguists agree that their dispersal might have been by infiltration rather than by large-scale migration (Crossland, 1971, pp. 828–29). A contrary proposition is now in vogue: that no language was ever replaced by another, at least before the era of large empires, from c. 500 BC onwards, unless substantial immigration introduced the new one. This theory is disproved by historical facts. We know that the Slaves who entered into Greece in the 6th century AD left hardly any archaeological trace (Hood, 1966).

A key question now is how early in prehistory 'elite dominance' or 'take over' by small groups of immigrants might have changed the language of an area with minimal cultural change. Such migrants might not always have had the new revolutionary techniques of warfare, e.g. the war-chariot (Crossland, 1971, pp. 873–74). In historical times populations living in ecologically marginal areas in mountains or deserts have regularly supplemented their resources by raiding more prosperous, settled neighbors, and moving into their territories. Regarding the time-scale of the differentiation of PIE, the present consensus is that 'glottochronology' has not proved reliable.

Krantz's attempt to explain the chronology of the introduction of different types of agriculture into various parts of Europe and the northern regions of the late U.S.S.R. is superficially plausible. His claim that genetic traits in modern Europeans support his conclusions is made in too little detail to assess (pp. 88–90). His conclusions that early Neolithic migrants into and within Europe spoke dialects or derivatives of PIE rests on two assumptions: that a language will rarely be introduced into an area without substantial immigration, and the idea that the differentiation of PIE into its historical descendants would have taken several millenia. Crossland doubts the last one on the basis of the development of Latin into medieval Romance languages in less than a thousand years. In general, his theory of a standard rate of advance for early farmers after the initial introduction of agriculture into Europe from Anatolia seems too schematic. He further argues that 'agriculture underwent a long period of development *in situ* in southeastern Europe, in which the people lived in the same settlement for several centuries.

Gamkrelidze & Ivanov work with a time-scale closer to that of the 'consensus' than is Krantz's with proto-Anatolian (the ancestor of Hittite and Luwian) diverging from PIE c. 4000 BC (1985a: 7). They postulate an IE homeland in eastern Anatolia, holding that similarities in vocabulary and grammar between IE, Semitic languages, and Kartvelian (Caucasic) imply that the Indo-Europeans learnt agriculture, including stock-breeding, from Semites, also that 'linguistic paleontology' points to a zone from the Balkans through Anatolia to northern Mesopotamia, with Armenia specially indicated. Crossland is of the view that the similarity in phonology and grammar suggests that "PIE developed in an area adjacent to the Caucasus". But Alice C. Harris, in When Worlds collide, has now questioned effectively the significance of most of them, and many of Gramkrelidze & Ivanov's identifications depend on their idiosyncratic reconstruction of the early IE system of stops. Others involve words that might have spread along trade-routes, e.g. 'peleku', 'axe', the word 'wine', and names of exotic animals. The 'linguistic paleontology' which supposedly points to Armenia is also dubious: even steppe-dwellers would have had words for 'mountain' and 'river' etc. The two authors posit a first IE migration into eastern and central Anatolia, introducing proto-

Anatolian there (1985b; 50–51); but Crossland thinks that loans from Hittite into Caucasian languages could have occurred as late as the 13th century BC. An argument against including central Anatolia in the homeland or a region of initial IE expansion is that a non-IE language, Hattic was the vernacular of Bagozkale-Hattusas and its vicinity c. 1700 BC. Hittite was then introduced at Hattusas as the spoken language of a new 'superstrate' and Hattic was also replaced by Palaic (IE and closely related to Hittite) in an adjacent area. Hattic was clearly a 'dead' language by the 14th century. Its preservation by the Hittites in religious cult suggests that it was not introduced into 'Hatti' recently, shortly before c. 1700 (Kammenhuber 1969, pp 125–38). The two languages were not juxtaposed much earlier. There was no extensive borrowing between them. Crossland (1971, pp. 844–5) is of the opinion that 'the loans were Hattic into Hittite, within 'Hatti', after c. 1700 BC. (Pre-) Hittite might have been brought into cappadocia from the west, not the east, by the 19th century (BC)'.

All the reconstructions that locate the homeland in Anatolia or east of it take some known IE peoples into their historical habitats by improbable routes; e.g. Gramkrelidze & lvanov have the proto-Greeks migrating across Anatolia after proto-Anatolian had settled there and bring them into Greece via Troad on the basis of an abandoned theory about the origin of Grey Minayan pottery. Crossland and other British linguists and archaeologists still prefer Gimbuta's reconstruction that 'in Neolithic times, as well as later, immigrants who achieved 'elite' status might well have introduced a new language into an area without significantly changing its material culture (Renfrew, 1988, p. 439; Anthony & Wales, 1988, p. 443). On the basis of linguistic studies of certain isoglosses (shared features) within sets of historical IE groups (including isolates like Greek) show a 'central–peripheral' distribution, which implies that the ancestors of the Celtic, Italic, and Anatolian groups and Tocharian left the continuum relatively early, while those of Greek, the Germanic, Baltic, Slavonic, and Indo-Iranian groups and Armenian remained in contact for longer, developing new shared features, before being dispersed (Crossland, 1971, pp. 863–7; 1982; 48–51). The ancestors of the 'peripheral' groups left the homeland earliest, in a radial pattern of emigration. The 'centum' system of dorsal stops would have been original, changing to 'satem' series in only some of the residual dialects. The Indo-Iranian migrations would have begun late. The process of dispersal indicated in consonants agrees with Gimbutas' view that 'Kurgan 1' people developed the precursor of PIE in the steppe region around 4000 BC or earlier. But it suggests that PIE as reconstructed by comparison evolved in an area of initial 'Kurgan' settlement in the Pontic region. Anthony & Wales have offered a new solution (1988, p. 443) that the Indo-Europeans should be identified as people of the Sredni Stog and Yamnaya cultures, just east of the Dnieper, c. 3800 BC who moved into the areas of the late Cucuteni-Tripolye and Gumelnitsa. This renewed appreciation of the importance of convergence processes in the formation of language, and of the view that family tree models, with a number of daughter languages diverging from a common proto-language is only appropriate in certain circumstances. As Dixon (1997) has stressed, in equilibrium periods, linguistic areas are built up by the diffusion of features, and rather different models are appropriate.

Renfrew has accepted the two criticisms against his theory of the dispersal of the Indo-European language from Anatolia to Europe as the result of a farming/language dispersal process associated with the spread of the neolithic way of life. The first criticism was about the emphasis on the "demic diffusion" model of Ammerman and Cavalli-Sforza (1973) for the spread of farming and that it would be more appropriate to think in terms of the adoption of farming by the indigenous population and of contact-induced language change (Zvelebil & Zvelbil, 1990, 1995). The second criticism was that the dispersal of a single language or proto-language was insufficient to account for the complexity of the patterning of the subsequent Indo-European languages, and that the account which had been offered was in linguistic terms too simplistic, too uni-dimensional, to carry plausibility. This too he accepted. In order to meet the two criticisms he has written this paper and had developed further the linguistic strata, and suggested that an 'important episode in the development of Proto-Indo-European was the emergence of a linguistic area in the Balkans in later Neolithic and Copper Ages (from around 5000 BC to 3000 BC) in precisely the area which Gimbutas sometimes referred to as "Old Europe" (Gimbutas, 1973)'.

Renfrew, in order to meet out the criticisms against his original theory of the dispersal of the Indo-European languages from Anatolia to far-off regions in a period extending from 6500 BC (Anatolia) to c. 2000 BC (Indo-Iranian), has now proposed four strata, by coining a new word 'pre-Proto-Indo-European' for the original language which developed in Archaic PIE and Proto-Anatolian (6500–5000 BC). In phase II (5000–3000 BC) he proposes that North and Northwestern PIE, Balkan PIE, and Early Steppe PIE emanated from the Archaic PIE of phase I. In phase III (3000–1500 BC), which he calls Late PIE, he suggests that Proto-Celtic and Proto-Germanic may have emanated from the North and Northwestern PIE: Proto-Baltic, Proto-Slavic, Proto-Greek, and Proto-Indo-Iranian etc. from Balkan PIE, both belonging to phase II. He is further of the opinion that Greek and Hittite emanated after 1500 BC from Proto-Greek of phase III and Proto-Anatolian of phase I, respectively.

Renfrew is quite conscious of the weakness of this suggestion when he says 'what is offered here is a framework, *with a palpable time depth* (emphasis mine), for Proto-Indo-European in place of the "flat" Proto-Indo-European commensurate with the specific homeland and single dispersal view and its later elaborations which generally accompany the hypothesis of a steppe dispersal around 3500 BC. He (Renfrew, 1999, p. 286) qualifies his suggestion by saying that:

> If the Indo-Hittite hypothesis is accepted and with it an Anatolian origin for early Proto-Indo-European then the spread of farming is the most obvious mechanism for the first stages (although of course other models cannot be excluded). This then requires a firm chronology, which can in fact readily be supplied by means of radiocarbon dating (although, as always, the claim to be dating linguistic phases rests on the assumption that these may indeed be correlated with archaeological ones).

He further accepts that 'The assessment of these proposal is primarily a matter for the competent linguists. It has not been my purpose here to set out original linguistic arguments.... The aim rather is to set out a framework which would be consistent with the information to be gleaned from the archaeological record and with the Indo-Hittite hypothesis, which linguists might find useful in establishing some sort of historical context for their work'. He further tries to substantiate his view by quoting Mallory (1997, 111):

If demic diffusion be limited to western Anatolia, the Balkans and Danubian Europe, and this be regarded as a linguistically interactive zone from the 7th to the 4th millennium BC, then it might be possible to envisage the dissemination of cultural terms within this region that are reconstructed to the proto-language.

Renfrew thinks that his 'hypothetical' proposals of the 'idea of Balkan Proto-Indo-European linguistic area, intermediate chronologically between an early Archaic phase and a late phase of Proto-Indo-European.... Would see the development of Indo-Iranian to the east and Proto-Celtic and Proto-Germanic to the west and north' finds support in the archaeological findings of Gimbutas 'Old Europe', although he is conscious of the fact that the 'Indo-Hittite hypothesis may invalidate in some respects her Kurgan theory'.

INDO-EUROPEAN LANGUAGES AND THE GREEK

In the period between the two world wars a vigorous debate began between the supporters and the opponents of the theory that many Greek words and many names of gods, heroes, men, and places in Greece were the remnants of one or more Indo-European languages distinct from Greek. The fact is that both sides have shown exaggeration in stating their positions. If we take all the hundreds of words and names which have at one time or the another been proposed as remnants of the pre-Greek Indo-European linguistic substratum, and if we discount all those which do not satisfy the rules of etymology, we are still left with ample evidence to support the theory that Indo-Europeans appeared in Greece before the arrival of the first Greek-speaking tribes, and enough information to help us determine some of the features which characterize the language or languages which they spoke. These are mainly phonetic. The Greek linguists have assigned to this substratum some of the suffixes also: *-s(s)-* (e.g. Kaukasa,

Marpesa, Amphissa, Antissa, Argissa, Larisa, Halikarnassos, Parnassos, Amnisos, Ilisos, Kephisos, Lykabettos, Hymettos, Kyparissos, narkisos); *anth-* and *-inth-* (e.g. Erymanthos, akanthos, Korinthos, terevinthos, hyakinthos, minthe); *-ymn-* and *-ynn-* (e.g. Kalymna, Larymna, Diktynna).

The philologists who specialize in tracing non-Greek elements of Indo-European origin in the Greek language do not agree about the number of original languages which must be postulated. According to the pioneer of this type of research, all non-Greek words are derived from a single language, conventionally referred to by them as "Pelasgic", which may have had two dialects. The other theory proposes that there were originally three main languages. The whole question remains open. The Greeks themselves regarded the Aones, Dryopians, Haimones, Hyantes, Kaukones, and Pelasgians as their predecessors, all having Indo-European names, and some of them can be connected with the civilizations of the Early and Middle Bronze Ages.

The sharp break in culture which marks the transition from the Early and Middle Bronze Ages in Thessaly and southern Mainland of Greece around 1900 BC was the result of the expansion of one section of the main body of Proto-Greeks into these lands from the regions where they had previously settled. One other group also moved into and got settled along the length of the Pindos Range and the axis of Epeiros-Aitolia. A third group was content to occupy the lands abandoned by the emigrants. There were no more migrations of Greeks on such a large scale and of such historical importance until the end of the Mycenean Age, c. 1150 BC. Thus, from 1900 to 1150 BC, the history of the formation of the Greek people followed an unbroken course.

The direct and indirect consequences of the large-scale migrations of about 1900 BC and of the smaller sporadic movements which followed are threefold:

(a) The earlier inhabitants were subdued, driven away, wiped out, or absorbed. Nevertheless, the Danaans in the Argolid and the Leleges in Eastern Lokris retained their independence up to the beginning of the Late Bronze Age; the Dryopians in the Spercheios Valley and the Kadmeians in

Boiotia held until the 13th century BC; the Abantes of Euboia remained autonomous until the end of the Bronze Age.

(b) The Proto-Greeks split up into groups; the individual characteristics of the original dialects multiplied, widening the distance between them so that new dialect branches were formed; many of the original tribes broke up, because they had become separated into smaller groups during the migration or for other reasons.

(c) The interchange of influences between the Proto-Greeks and the earlier population led to cultural proximity; in some cases, the Proto-Greeks completely absorbed the earlier inhabitants; in other cases, new combinations were formed out of the mingling of exclusively Proto-Greek elements.

The first two developments resulted eventually in the transformation of the Proto-Greek tribes into the Greek tribes of the Mycenean Age. In alphabetical order, these were: the Arbantes, Achaians, Ainianes, Aiolians, Aithikes, Aitolians, Arkadians, Arktanes, Athamanians, Boiotians, Dolopes, Dorians, Epeians, Graioi, Hellenes, Ionians, Kephallenians, Kouretes, Lapiths, Lokrians, Macedonians, Magnetes, Minyans, Molossians, Myrmidons, Per(rh)aibians, Phlegyans, Phokians, Phthians, Pierians, Thesprotians, and Thessalians.

Thus, it is clear that there is definite evidence of the spread of the Indo-European in Greece. As far as the Hellenic branch of the Indo-European is concerned, it is clear that they destroyed the Minoan civilization and that they mastered the art of the people they subjugated (Misra, 1992, p. 101). Thus the Greeks were invaders and came to Greece from outside. There is a vast substratum of pre-Greek languages and culture on which was foisted at a later date the Hellenic civilization of the early Greeks.

INDIA—THE 'HOMELAND' OF INDO-EUROPEAN LANGUAGES?

I have given above the history of Indo-European studies somewhat in detail in order to see as to how the world of western scholarship had been, and is still, engaged in denying any place to Indian subcontinent being the original homeland of IE languages. They have been putting forward various theories (both archaeological and linguistic) to show that this language could not have originated in India, although they are themselves not sure as to where it could have originated. I am trying to state here the latest archaeological discoveries and studies in Indian subcontinent and the western Asia which are in agreement with the known historical facts of the distribution of IE languages in Eurasia.

The French archaeologist, Jean Francois Jarrige, has conducted an outstandingly successful excavation at the site of Mehargarh in Baluchistan (W. Pakistan) and there is now evidence for the cultivation of cereal crops (Six-rowed barley, Einkorn, Emmer, and bread-wheat) in 7000–6000 BC (Mallory and Adams 1997, 308). Besides Mehargarh in the North-West, we have evidence of cultivation of rice (*oryza sativa*) in c. sixth millennium BC at Koldihwa-Mahagara in Allahabad district of U.P. (Allchin, 1982, p. 110) and of cross-furrowed cultivated field in the pre-Harappan context (c. 3000 BC) in the dried-up beds of the Vedic river Saraswati in Hanumangarh district of Rajasthan. In addition to archaeological evidences we have certainly enough references in the Vedic texts as to how the society developed from the nomadic-semi-nomadic and pastoral stage to village settlements. It would be interesting to note the references to cities and city-life in early Vedic texts. There are abundant references to agriculture and agricultural-equipment in these texts. It is absolutely clear from the study of the geographical data available in the Rigveda that the North-West was the nuclear zone of the Rigvedic Aryans and the whole theory of the Indo-Europeans coming to India is based upon a surmise that the Indus Valley people were non-Aryans. But who knows that the people of the Indus Valley civilization could already have been speaking an Indo-European language? The script when deciphered may prove this conjecture or may disprove it? However, we do find the traces of various elements of the Hindu religion in the religious life of the Indus people, e.g., the worship of phallus, water, tree, Pashupat-Shiva etc. Thus, it seems to be clear that IE homeland was in or near northwest India and that the other IE languages had emigrated from this region. Mallory simply conjectures 'Proto-Indo-Aryan farmers with introducing agriculture to India' (1997, p. 308).

Raymond and Bridget Allchin considered the case of pre-vedic movements into the plains of India and Pakistan. Pointing to distinctive fireplaces at the site of Kalibanga, which may be interpreted as ritual hearths, they say:

> Such ritual hearths are reported from the beginning of the Harappan period itself. It has been suggested that they may have been fire-altars, evidence of domestic, popular and civic fire-cults of the Indo-Iranians, which are described in detail in the later Vedic literature. It may then be an indication of culture contact between an early group of Indo-Aryans and population of the still flourishing Indus Civilization.

Allchins (1982) do not suggest that the Indus Civilization itself should be regarded as Indo-European speaking, but simply the elements within it may already be recognized which is later characteristic of Indo-Aryan culture, as seen in the Rigveda.

But, since the development of the civilization can quite plausibly be traced right back to early roots in the findings at Mehargarh, the origin of the Neolithic there is of greatest relevance. The difficulty, of course, is that the area in question is a long way south and east of the recognized early farming cultures in the Zagros. Why is it not plausible to think that the development of agriculture from the mesolithic hunting-gathering stage at Mehargarh was an indigenous affair? Why should it be concluded that it was a dispersal from Iraqi-Kurdistan, as Mallory suggests (1997, p. 309)?

Renfrew suggests two hypotheses for the identification of Indo-Aryans in India:

Hypothesis A : Neolithic Arya.
Hypothesis B : Mounted Nomads of the Steppes.

He suggests that the successors of the eastern Anatolian languages were Indo-Iranian languages and that the original separation would have taken place by 6500 BC, because he believes in the Anatolian homeland of agriculture, and, therefore, of the Indo-European languages. He further suggests three cultural and economic processes for the dispersal of Indo-Iranian languages:

(i) Colonization by early peasant farmers of Iran and Pakistan (Mehargarh).
(ii) Development of nomad pastoralism in the Steppe lands of Russia, i.e. dispersal from west to east (presence of horse in the 3rd Millennium BC in Central Asia).
(iii) Elite dominance, where well-organized communities of mounted nomad pastorals, with a ranked social organization, achieved dominance in certain areas by force of arms in the first and second millennium BC as we have no evidence for mounted warriors at an earlier time.

As is clear from the above discussions in connection with PIE phases I and II of Renfrew, none of the models suggested by him fits well even in the archaeology of central Asia and south-central Europe ("Old Europe" of Gimbutas). So far as India is concerned his first hypothesis of Neolithic Arya (if by it he means an agricultural community who could be responsible for the origin of Indo-European language!) is well attested both archaeologically and by the Vedic texts. If the evidence of agriculture in the sixth-seventh millennium BC in Anatolia could be the reason for the origin of IE languages there, and their dispersal in various hypothetical phases in the various parts of Eurasia, why could India be not accepted as the original homeland of this language group where we have the living continuous tradition of this language. If it originated in Anatolia then why do we not find any text of this language there having an antiquity as the Vedas have? Probably the language survived in India due to the concern of ancient Vedic seers to keep it intact in its purest form by developing various schools of philosophy entirely devoted to the preservation of the purity of the language (*vyakarana*, *Mimamsa and Nyaya*). We do not find any such concern in the western world even today. They became interested in the philosophy of language in the 20th century, and not in the study of language itself. Linguistic taxonomy has been their concern and not the language as such, probably because they wish to disprove that their own languages emanated from some other group of people, and that it developed indigenously. Greek, the ancient most European language, from which all the European languages emanate, does not have any text prior to Homer (c. 600 BC) except the Linear B tablets having some words connected with trade and commerce supposedly belonging to the 12th century BC. Had IE languages emanated in Anatolia it would have dispersed to Greece in the very early phase (phase 1 or 2 of Renfrew) because Greece is geographically closer and have many close similarities in cultural traits with the Neolithic and Bronze Age cultures of Western Asia, instead of reaching south-central Europe in 5000–3000 BC? I wish to mention here that most of the cosmogonical symbols available in the archaeology of the "Old Europe" belong to the Vedic literature (Tripathi, 2000, P.1ff.) rather than to any of the Anatolian or Western Asiatic text or Greek texts.

For deciding the homeland of the IE language we have to keep the following important points in our mind:

(i) The dichotomy between the Vedic and the Indus culture does not exist now.

(a) Both the Raos-Krishna and Surya- from their reading of the Indus script have concluded that the script is proto-Brahmi and its contents Purano-Vedic. This has most recently been confirmed by an independent study of German scholar Egbert Richter-Ushanas (*Times of India*, New Delhi, dated February 13, 1999). He says that there is "basic equivalence" of the inscriptions on the Indus seals and the Rig Veda.

(b) On the basis of the archaeological and literary evidences both Hazra and Bhattacharya have suggested that the Indus Valley Culture is an Aryan Culture. The evidence of horse bones from Surkotda (c. 2455–1860 BC), spoked wheels from Harappa, and many other religious practices common to both is enough to prove that both the cultures belong to one cultural-milieu rather than being different cultures.

(ii) Aryan names have been found in the documents of Mitanni, Nuzi, and Khattis (Hittites). At least 81 Aryan proper names (13 from Mitanni, 23 from Nuzi, and 45 from Syrian documents) are known. They are precisely dated in the 2nd–3rd millennia BC.

(a) The Mitannian have king Tusharatta (i.e. Dasaratha) who worships Raman (Rama) as his family deity (vide letter of Tusaratta to Amenhotep III, dated in c. 1400 BC in the Tell-el-Amarna archives).

(b) A treatise on the training of horses has been found in the Bogazkeui archives (c. 1400 BC). It is written by one Kikkuli, a Hittite horse trainer in Sanskrit language. (See Appendix I).

(c) Finally, the Bogazkeui treaty (1380 BC) between the Hittite king Supplilulium and the Mitanni king Mattiwaza, invokes the Vedic gods Indra, Varuna, Mitra, and Nasatyas as guardian of the treaty. P. Thieme holds that they were Indian and not Indo-Iranian deities.

(iii) Date of the Rigveda. (See Appendix II)

(a) Though no final date for the Rigveda is available on firm grounds, yet it is unanimously agreed upon that it is the first extant literature of mankind. On the basis of astrological calculations the date of the *Satapatha Brahman* has been fixed in 3000 BC by S.B. Dixit. Thibeau finds a mistake of one thousand years in the calculation. In any case, the date of the Rigveda will have to be placed in the fourth–third millennia BC, if the astrological calculations have any meaning.

(b) If the Indus Valley culture is to be identified with the Aryan culture in India then, also, the date of the Rigveda will have to be placed in pre-3000 BC, as the earliest radiocarbon date of the Indus Civilization is now placed in 3100–3200 BC.

(c) The date of the Bogazkeui inscription is firmly fixed in 1386 BC. If the names of the Rigvedic deities occur on it then the Rigveda has to be dated long before that date because the concept of divinities does not prop up all of a sudden. It must have taken a long time before they could have occupied an important place in the minds of the people and their importance were recognized by the two western Asian states and their people.

(d) The archaeological data available from the "Old Europe", firmly dated by radiocarbon method in 6th–5th millennia BC, definitely proves that all the cosmogonical images available there have Vedic contexts (Tripathi, 2000).

(e) Even if we accept the European model of the dispersal of IE languages with the dispersal of agriculture, evidences available from Mehargarh are sufficient proofs that the language in discussion must have originated in the Indian subcontinent.

(f) Lal (2002, p. 136) has recently argued the case of the antiquity and cultural continuity of India and has come to the conclusion that it has 'its roots deep in antiquity, some seven to eight thousand years ago, and its flowering in the third millennium BC, still lives on, not as a fugitive but as a vital organ of our socio-cultural fabric.'

I am aware of the fact that the proposal stated above will not be palatable to many of the western scholars (and their followers in India, as well!). What I wish to reiterate here is that any model suggested by them does not exclude India being the homeland of the Indo-European languages. Once you are ready to examine the question dispassionately, archaeological, linguistic, and textual information available in India definitely suggests India being the "homeland" of this language. If India, with its living texts of great antiquity and unbroken cultural tradition could not be the homeland then none of the places suggested could be taken seriously to be the homeland of this language.

APPENDIX I: HITTITE AN INDO-EUROPEAN LANGUAGE

Hittite	*Greek/Latin*	*Sanskrit*	*Meaning*
Genu	Genu	Janu	Knee
Kwish	Quis	Kim	Who
Hastai	Osteo	Asthi	Bone
Hanti	Anti	Han, Hanti	Against/Kill
Akw	Acqua	XXXXX	Water
Pahhur	Pyre	XXX	Pyre

MITANNI : AN INDO-ARYAN LANGUAGE

Mitanni	*Sanskrit*	*Meaning*
Mitrasil	Mitra	God Mitra
Nasattayana	Nasatyau	Twin Nasatya Gods
Arunasil	Varuna	God Varuna
Indar	Indra	God Indra
Aik-Wartanna	Ekavartanam	One Round
Tera-Wartanna	Trivartanam	Three Rounds
Pancha-Wartanna	Panchavartanam	Five Rounds
Satta-Wartanna	Saptavartanam	Seven Rounds
Nava-Wartanna	Navavartanam	Nine Rounds

APPENDIX II: DATE OF THE RIGVEDA

1. Swami Daya Nand Saraswati[1]	Since the beginning of creation.
2. Das, A.C.	25,000 years BP.
3. Tilak, B.G.	8000–7000 BC.
4. Shankar Balakrishna Dixit	6000 BC.
5. Gupta, S.P.	5000 BC.
6. Jacobi, Hermann	4500–2500 BC.
7. Winternitz, H.[7]	2500 BC.

1. *Rigvedadi Bhasya Bhumika*, 1991, pp. 9–26, Delhi (Offset).
2. *Rigvedic Culture of India*, 1922, Calcutta.
3. *The Orion or Researches in the antiquity of the Vedas*, 4th edition, 1955, Poona, p. 27.
4. *Bharatiya Jyotisha Shastra*, 1963, pp. 136–140.
5. *The "Lost" Saraswati and Indus Civilization*, Kusumanjali Prakashan, Jodhpur, 1995.
6. See in Winternitz, M.: *History of Indian Literature, 2 Vols.*, Oriental Books, New Delhi, 1972 (Reprint), pp. 294–300.
7. Ibid.

CHAPTER 3

The Concept of Man and Humanism

CONCEPT OF MAN AND HUMANISM IN INDIAN TRADITION

Background

What does humanity mean? The search for a definition of man has been going on since time immemorial. Modern concept of *Homo-Economicus* leads to fractionalization of man and loss of humanity. Hence, moral regeneration of man, going beyond *amour propre* and developing concerns for the well-being of others, is being recognized as an essential element by the present world. It is necessary to return to classical perspectives, both Hellenism and Hinduism, which consider man as a composite entity of body–mind–soul and its order being the basis of humanity. Both in Hellenism and Hinduism man is a self-complete entity and is an integral part of the cosmos. It is also the mode of coupling the finite with the absolute and this coupling forms the basis of values and meaning in the light of which men can refashion the givens of nature (including their own) and society. This examination does not mean going back to the order of things as associated with the tradition in the past—it is neither possible nor desirable. This examination is simply meant to disconceal the insight that undergird these world-views. It is this insight—that is, insight into the structure of order—that can open the horizon of the future and provide guidelines for restructuring man and his world.

Meaning of the term Humanism

Different currents of the idea of Humanism are to be seen in the western world. We have different shades of this term in the contemporary humanistic view of man (T. Servin, Corliss Lamont, John R. Platt, and William James). Views of behavioral scientists (Hubert Bonner, Erich Fromm, James F.T. Bugental, Rollo May and Abraham, H. Maslow) and that of the natural scientist (J. Bronowski) differ sharply from each other. Lamont (1965) presents the latest modern definition of this term. Two modern humanist traditions—the Mainstream and the Minority—are clearly visible in the western world.

However, in Indian tradition, it is not rationality, as in Aristotle, but morality (*dharma*) that differentiates man from other animals. Realization that the pleasures of the body, even reject the existence of the soul which, as the sensorium of the divine, has the necessary attributes to lift man from his status as *anyarat* or which Plato calls the 'servitude of many mad masters'. Only when the soul is attuned to the divine ground of being that it does become capable of discriminating between what is worth doing and what is not in a particular context of action. It is only then that man becomes *swarat* and does well to himself and to all. Man must transcend his narrow self-interest, only then can he relate himself to others. The source of *dharma* cannot be any human or divine authority and that the source of knowledge of *dharma,* the distinguishing feature of man, can be found in some transcendental internality as *atma-tushti.* The ideal of liberation consists in the realization by the soul of its pristine purity or essential perfection. The humanistic implication of the doctrine of *Jivanmukti* is obvious. The highest perfection or fulfillment of which man is capable of can be attained and enjoyed by him here in his earthly existence. In India (*Advaita Vedanta*) the *Atman* within is elevated to the status of the First Principle of the Universe and nothing superior to man exists in the universe (*Mahabharata*). We find references to humanism as early as in the Rigveda in the form of three civil liberties of *tana* (*body*), *Skridhi* (*dwelling-houses*), *and Jibasi* (*life*), and the affirmation of the identity of *Atman* and *Brahman* as well as the doctrine of *Mukti* or salvation and the difference between *preya* and *shreya* is clearly indicated in the Upanishads. The law of Karma stresses the fact of the soul's independence of god and the ideal of *Jivanmukti,* liberation in the worldly life. The impact of Vedanta on the medieval and modern Indian thought is clearly visible in the *Navya-Nyaya* of medieval Indian mind and in the 19th century Renaissance led by Raja Rammohun Roy, Swami Daya Nand Saraswati, Devendra Nath Tagore, Ramkrishna Paramhans and Swami Vivekanand.

Buddhism is also a humanistic religion. Buddha did neither believe in God, nor, in the Vedas or a Prophet. He preached to his followers to believe in only such pronouncements, which are logical and tested on, lived experiences. *Nirvana* can be attained in this life (cf. *Jivanmukti*). The belief in the law *of karma* and belief in *Bodhisattva* form an important ingredient of the Buddhist concept of humanism. *Ahimsa* as the main constituent of righteousness or *dharma* clearly represents humanism.

Tradition of Humanism in medieval and modern Indian thought is seen in Vaishnavism which preached equality of all men; in fact all the saints of the Bhakti movement believed in it. The Sudras, the helots of the ancient Hindu, preached shoulder to shoulder with the Brahmin (who welcomed and encouraged it), when the God of the Hindu was for the first time worshipped with hymns composed by a Mohammadan (*Rasakhana*) and when Ramadasa declared that man is free and he cannot be subjected by force (*Naradeha swadhina; sahasa na hve paradhina, Das-bodha,I,10.25*). Two Secularist Humanists of the 20th century India are M.N. Roy and Jawahar Lal Nehru; and, Rabindra Nath Tagore and Mahatma Gandhi may be designated as religious humanists.

To sum up, the modern age is said to be facing a crisis—a civilizational crisis—of a very great magnitude. This crisis, known as a modern *problematique*, to use a French phrase, represents the accumulated follies of mankind in the last three hundred years. The one solution to the crisis that is frequently alluded to is a return to humanism. The trouble, however, is that humanism has different connotations, different meanings, and different referents. A responsible and serious philosopher of humanism should occupy himself with the questions and queries about values that have agitated and intrigued the human mind through the ages. India, indeed, has, intellectually, a relatively maturer tradition of religious thought than the Semitic and Christian world. Here, centuries before Christ, Mahavira, and Gautam Buddha, as also the founders of the *Samkhya* system, propounded religious philosophies not committed to the belief in a creator God. Indian religious tradition, thus, may claim to be more varied, more liberal, and tolerant. Modern humanism can, therefore, derive inspiration and support from India's cultural tradition.

Humanism is a word which is used by writers in philosophy in many different senses. One of these implies that man makes up the entire framework of human thought that there is no God, no superhuman Reality to which he can be related or can relate himself. It is obviously *not* in this sense that I am using the term here. I am using the word here in the sense that anyone who attaches the highest value to man and all that pertains to him—his values, his ideals, his intelligence, his creativity, his social welfare—is a humanist, without eliminating God as irrelevant. This attempt will unite rather than divide. The attempt should be to see the unity in diversity, the common factors in apparent dualism. It is not possible to find instances of unadulterated humanistic philosophy in ancient and medieval cultural traditions, eastern or western.

True humanism should not be reluctant or unwilling to exclude any important human concern or institution that has played a significant role in man's cultural history from its purview. Even today religion remains a force to be reckoned with and only a few intellectuals in the West claiming to be humanist feel compelled to severe their connection from orthodox Christianity.

The basic question facing the humanist is: can humanism find a way to preserve and defend the best in the moral and spiritual traditions of mankind without invoking supernatural authority? In order to find an answer to this question we shall have to examine the history of humanistic thought in the classical Indian tradition.

The Conceptual Structure of Classical Indian Thought about Man

The concepts relating to the study and understanding of man in the Indian tradition may be approached in different ways. One such approach is to consider the differentiating characteristic of man that sets him apart from all other beings, particularly those of the animal kingdom with whom he shows such an obvious affinity. What, in other words, is his *vyavartaka laksana*? The most general answer is that it is *dharma*, the self-conscious awareness of the distinction between "is" and "ought", coupled with a consciousness that the "ought" should be desired and willed, implying thereby that man has the capacity to effectuate what he perceives or apprehends as his *dharma*. A well-known utterance in this regard is:

Dharmena hinah pasubhih samanah.
(Devoid of *dharma*, man is just like other animals).

It is therefore not rationality, as Aristotle regards, but morality that differentiates man from other animals.

The definition of man as a moral being is not to characterize him as being essentially moral, but rather to suggest that he is a being who inevitably *judges* all actions, whether his own or those of others, as right or wrong, evil or virtuous, or that it would have been better if the 'right' action had been done rather than the 'wrong' one, and that this consciousness does not, and cannot ever leave him for it characterizes him as a special human being and not just as this or that person.

But how does he *know* what right or wrong is, or what *dharma* is? For, if *dharma* is the feature that distinguishes humans from other living forms it is imperative that one finds what characterizes *dharma* and how it is known. The classical answer to the first question is that *dharma* consists of *vidhi* and *nishedha*, that is, what should be done and what should not be done. *Kartavyata* is at the heart of it, but as hypothetical imperatives are accepted as *dharma*, even in the context of the Vedas, conditionality is not excluded from the notion of *dharma*. Not only this, the notion of *dharma* varies in relation to *varna, asrama, jati, kula, desa, kala, yuga*, and ultimately even with the individual person concerned. There is, of course, the notion of *sadharana dharma* which is binding upon all human beings, but between *svadharma* and *sadharana dharma* there are other *dharmas* that affect and modify both, sometimes in contradictory ways. As Yudhisthira, the very embodiment of *dharma*, says in a particular context in the *Mahabharata:* 'There are times when doing what is regarded as *dharma* becomes an act of *adharma*, and doing what is considered *adharma* becomes the real *dharmic* act in the situation'. But whatever the problems about the specificity of *dharma* in a particular context or situation, its formal character remains the same, that is, it is always an injunction or a prohibition, a *vidhi* or a *nishedha*.

As for the question of how *dharma* is to be known, the answer is that it cannot be known either by perception or inference, the normal sources of knowledge. Yet, if *dharma* is the distinguishing feature of man and if usual processes employed for acquiring knowledge cannot know it, we have to postulate a distinctive source other than perception or inference. This is usually described as *sabda* and *sruti* in the tradition. But it would make better understanding if the two were kept apart and not confused with each other. *Sabda* need not necessarily be *apaurusheya*, as *sruti* is supposed to be, it can be a *Pramana* for believing in the veracity of ordinary, empirical descriptive statements which *sruti*, both in its *Jaimini* and *Badarayana* interpretations, is not supposed to be.

Sruti then is different from *sabda*. Although both are important for knowledge of *dharma*, *sruti* is more basic and fundamental than *sabda* in its wider and generally accepted meaning. But what is a *sruti* and why is it supposed to give us knowledge of *dharma*? A new concept is introduced at this stage to characterize an aspect of *dharma* that makes it specifically fit to be known by *sruti*. This is the concept of *adrishta*, something that cannot be apprehended by the senses or the reason. *Dharma* is supposed to have this character of *adrishta* in two senses: the first may be put in modern terminology and may appear to the modern mind as more fundamental. This is the non-derivability of 'ought' from 'is'. If this is accepted, it will easily be seen why *dharma* which consists of 'do's and 'don'ts', or *vidhi* and *nishedha*, cannot be perceived, as it is not a sensible object or derived from it through any reasoning, unless there be somewhere in the premises at least one premise which itself is imperative in nature. *Sruti*, in this perspective, would be that foundational imperative or set of imperatives from which all other imperatives are derived. This is somewhat akin to the notion of *grundnorm* formulated by Kelsen, a status that is generally accorded to the constitution of a country in the constitutional law, or is regarded as natural law in the context of *adrishta* or law in general.

The second aspect relates to what may be called non-empirical causality, that is, where the assertion of *Karanata* is of such a nature that it cannot, in principle, be verified in the usual way and yet whose postulation is required to make the world morally intelligible to actors who feel obliged to act according to the demands of *dharma.* This is the problem of the relation between 'morality' and 'happiness' in the Kantian terms, or between *Yajna and svarga* in the language of *Jaimini.* The source of *dharma* cannot be any human or divine authority for then that authority would become superior to *dharma*, whether or not it declares itself to be so (cf. *Gita*: '*saravan dharman parityajya mam ekam saranam vrajet*). Action, according to *dharma,* must lead to a *Phala* or result which is acceptable to the 'moral sensibility' of man, even though *dharma* is not followed for the sake of that result, and in actual fact is seldom seen to be associated with it.

Sruti, however, is regarded in the tradition as the *only* source of acquiring knowledge about *dharma.* But, Manu cites three other sources which he calls *smriti, sadachara, and atma-tusti*. The source of knowledge of *dharma*, the distinguishing feature of man, may thus be found in some transcendental internality as *atma-tusti.*

The doctrine of *purushartha* points to both the empirical and transcendental nature of man as it includes not only *dharma* and *moksha* as *purusharthas*, but also *artha* and *kama* amongst the legitimate ends which man ought to pursue if he has to fulfill his nature as human being. This empirical–transcendental nature of human being leads to an analysis in terms of his body, mind, intellects, and ego or the sense of 'I' on the one hand, and consciousness or self or *purusha or atman*, on the other. There is further division of *sthula and sukshma* or gross and subtle at almost all levels from the body to the ego or 'I', on the one hand, and between *sattvika, rajasika,* and *tamasika,* deriving from the threefold *Samkhyan* classification of *Prakriti*, on the other. To be embodied is to be *Jiva*, and to be a *jiva* is, by definition, to be in a state characterized by *avidya* which is supposed to be the cause of bondage.

Thus, the complex of *chita, ahamkara* or the sense of ego, *buddhi* or intellect, *manasa* or mind, and the *indriyas* or the senses, constitutes the *jiva* or the embodied being which at the human level is differentiated by the capacity to discriminate between *dharma* and *adharma*, *sat* and *asat*, and *nitya* and *anitya*. It is born and it dies, like all beings in the world, and like other living beings is capable of feeling *sukha* and *duhkha*, that is, pleasure and pain, and like them, seeks the former and shuns the latter. But, unlike all other beings, the *Viveka* that he alone has, coupled with the fact that he enjoys a *karma-yoni* which gives him the freedom to seek not only pleasure but that which is *sat*, *nitya*, and *dharmic* in nature, gives him a unique status envied by all other beings in the universe.

India is one of the few civilized lands where philosophies of liberation divorced from theistic belief in a creator God were expounded and elaborated. It was here, again, that the grand system of *Advaita Vedanta*, elevating the *Atman* within to the status of the first principle of the universe, was systematically developed, and the doctrine of *Jivanmukti* (liberation-in-life here on earth) was placed on secure metaphysical foundations in several systems of thought. Here, indeed, the author of the great epic *Mahabharata*, the encyclopaedia of Indian moral and spiritual thought, felt free to proclaim: *Nothing superior to man exists.*

India, indeed, has intellectually a relatively mature tradition of religious thought than the Semitic and Christian world. Here, centuries before Christ, Mahavira, and Gautam Buddha as also the founders of the *Sankhya* system propounded religious philosophies not committed to belief in a creator God. Indian religious tradition may claim to be more varied, more liberal and tolerant. *This is one reason why modern humanism can derive inspiration and support from India's cultural tradition.* Another reason is the peculiar metaphysical conception of liberation or perfection elaborated by the more important philosophical systems of this land. A responsible and serious philosopher of humanism should occupy himself with the questions and queries about values that have agitated and intrigued through the ages.

Indian tradition is particularly rich in suggestions for the reconstruction of the religious attitude along the humanistic lines.

Even today religion remains a force to be reckoned with. There may be very few intellectuals in the West claiming to be humanist feel compelled to severe their connection from Orthodox Christianity.

Upanishadic-Vedantic Humanism: The Metaphysical Roots

In the extensive literature of the Upanishads, the Indian mind shows its first awareness of the problem of the nature and destiny of man. The number of the Upanishads is too large, but only about thirteen of these are taken to be authoritative and authentic, being genuine parts of the Vedic literature. These uphold the non-dualistic or monistic view of reality, the *Advaitic* trend.

The aforesaid awareness is not to be met in the pre-Upanishadic texts, the Vedas proper and the *Brahmanas*. The hymns of the Vedas, the oldest amongst which is the *Rigveda*, represent the sentiments, attitudes, and beliefs of the people with simple minds yet uncorrupted by inconvenient questionings and undisturbed by troublesome doubts. Not that the authors of Vedic hymns do not ask questions at all; these questions, however, relate mostly to gods and goddesses and, on some rare occasions, to the architect or creator and the creation of the world. Throughout their reflections, however, their attention continued to be directed on things outside the human world, those circumstances which prevented them from specifically raising the questions concerning the nature and destiny of man himself. The Universe as conceived by them does not assign any important place to man. On the other hand, the earthly life constitutes the central concern of the Vedic Aryans. Should this latter attitude towards life be called humanistic? Perhaps not, for it is neither rooted in, nor supported by the peculiar world-view entertained by them.

Transition to the Upanishads

The Upanishads, particularly the more important among them, mark a two-fold break or departure from the world-view and the values entertained and cherished by the authors of the *Atharvaveda* and the *Brahmanas:* (*a*) The primary concern of the Upanishads is the affirmation of the identity of *Atman* and *Brahman*, and not relation of the story of creation or sacrificial practices. This was a tremendous achievement. The idea has long been a blasphemy and heresy to Christianity and to this day to official Islam. Compare: The 'divination of man was at first made tentatively and hesitatingly. Throughout the late Middle Ages and much of the Renaissance it was accompanied by recurrent feelings of bad conscience. In the thirteenth century the sense of blasphemy was still meditated by a strong apprehension of God's presence in all things. But the fourteenth century generally envisaged God as a real but absent Governor of the Universe, and this endowed the human confiscation of the divine attributes with the character of rebellion, punishable by eternal damnation' etc.

This may, among other things, be taken as indicating a shift toward the subjective as against the preoccupation with the objective—the external world and its ruling powers, the gods and the goddesses, the *Purusha*, *Prajapati*, *Vishwakarma or Hirnyagarbha*—which was the characteristic of the Vedas and the Brahmanas. Voicing this subjective bias, the *Brihadaranyaka Upanishad* (LI. 4.5) recommends (a) 'The *Atman* alone is to be seen, to be heard and thought about and meditated upon'; (b) The realization that the cult of sacrifice cannot lead us to the goal of liberation or the highest fulfillment. *Mundaka Upanishad* in an oft-quoted stanza (1.2.7) characterizes the sacrifice as frail boats. 'Fool they are', it goes on to declare, 'who call these the highest good; again and again they fall into the clutches of old age and death'.

The Upanishadic View of Self

Following are the characteristic features of the Upanishadic view of self:

(1) The soul or self (*Atman*) is both unborn and imperishable.
(2) All Vedantic *acharyas* (i.e., philosopher-teachers who base their doctrines on the Upanishads, *Bhagavadgita*, and the *Brahma Sutras*, the so-called *Prasthanatrayi*) believe in the law of *karma* and the theory of transmigration of the soul from one form of life to another in accordance with its moral

deserts. (Cf. *Chhandogya Upanishad* (V.10.7); *Brihadaranyaka Upanishad* (III.2.13); *Kathaka Upanishad* (V.7), etc.)

(3) All Vedantic *acharyas* agree in declaring the highest goal of life to be liberation *or Mukti* from the round of births and deaths.

(4) The doctrine of *Mukti* or salvation: The more important Upanishads draw a distinction between *preya* and *sreya*, worldly prosperity and the highest good consisting in liberation or *mukti* from *samsara.*

Humanistic implications of the Upanishadic view of the soul or self

(1) The individual soul, according to the Upanishads, is unborn and immortal. In other words, souls owe neither their being nor their continued existence to God. The conception of the soul as an imperishable eternal entity obviously involves its ontological independence. Judaism, Christianity, and Islam may contrast with this notion of the soul that propagated. All these religions consider the soul to be a created entity deriving its being from God; they also believe that the continued existence of the soul depends on the sweet will of god who can destroy it if he so wills or desires. Needless to say the *Advaita Vedanta*, which identifies the soul with Brahman, declares it to be the highest principle in the universe.

(2) The law of *karma* stresses the fact of soul's independence of god in another direction. God cannot punish or penalize the soul without reference to its moral past. God cannot interfere with the working of the law of *karma.* In fact, according to Hindu mythology, even the gods are subject to the inexorable law of *karma*. Destiny is largely independent of god. In addition to Jainism and Buddhism, the philosophical schools of *Purva Mimamsa* and *Sankhya* do not accept the authority of god.

(3) These Hindu Schools of thought are taken to be orthodox for the reason that they subscribe to the authority of the Vedas.

(4) It is noteworthy that both the heretical creeds of Jainism and Buddhism and the atheistic philosophies of *Sankhya-Yoga* and the *Purva Mimamsa* subscribe to belief in the ultimate salvation, liberation or *mukti*. Buddhism however, does not believe in any eternal entity like the soul; nevertheless, it believes in the ultimate goal of *mukti* or *nirvana*. Practically all classical systems of Indian philosophy, orthodox and heterodox, are inclined to equate liberation with self-realization. The conclusion is that *mukti* or liberation consists in the realization by the soul of its own pristine purity or essential perfection.

(5) Another important aspect of the Upanishadic view, which finds fuller development in the hands of later philosophers, is a belief in the possibility of liberation-in-life, sole evidence of which consists in the observable peace and tranquility that characterize one's life. This doctrine of *Jivanmukti*, in one form or the other, is accepted by most of the classical philosophers including the Jain and the Buddhist thinkers. The humanistic implications of the doctrine of *Jivanmukti* are obvious. The highest perfection or fulfillment of which man is capable of can be attained and enjoyed by him here in his earthly existence.

The humanistic side of Upanishadic metaphysics finds clearer expression in Sankara and his followers:

(a) The doctrine of the self-luminosity of the self is the cornerstone of the Advaitic metaphysics (*Svayamprakash*);

(b) Brahman is accessible to us in our own being or self. Metaphysically speaking, Brahman can be reached only through the *Atman*;

(c) The entire panorama of phenomenal existence belongs to the realm of *Maya*, the principle of cosmic illusion;

(d) The role of the *pramanas* including the scriptures is limited to removing the veil of ignorance or *avidya*. *Bhagavadgita* (II.46) agrees with this view. Gautama, Kanada, and Kapila developed their philosophical concepts without reference to scriptural texts. Kabir, Dadu Dayal, Raidas, Guru Nanak and in our own times Ramkrishna Paramhamsa developed their own philosophies without any knowledge of the Vedantic Texts. Like Aristotle, Sankara seems to exalt the life of contemplation over that of action, but the sort of contemplation envisaged by him is closely allied to meditation.

BUDDHISM: A HUMANISTIC RELIGION

Among the greatest religions of the world, Buddhism probably has a greater claim to be called humanistic than any other religion. While the great Chinese thinkers, Lao-tse and Confucius, have pronounced humanistic leanings, they are not averse to indulging in metaphysical speculations which Buddha avoided in his teachings. On the other hand, Confucianism may claim to be more purely ethical in its emphasis than Buddhism wherein the goal of *Nirvana* receives as much, if not more, emphasis as virtuous life leading to it.

Gautam Buddha (563–483 BC) is unique among the great founders of religions in more ways than one:

(a) He did not claim either to be the message bearer of an Omniscient God or to be the vehicle of a revealed scripture.
(b) He did not claim to be an omniscient teacher whose words should be accepted as a matter of faith.
(c) He was inclined to look upon experience both as the source and as the touchstone of truth.
(d) He asked his followers not to accept his words as being divinely inspired but to weigh and test his pronouncements against logic and with reference to actual, lived experience or life (cf. *Anguttara Nikaya,* Part III: dialogue between Buddha and the Kalamas).
(e) Again, like the Upanishadic sages, Buddha believes that the condition of *Nirvana* can be attained and experienced by the aspirant here in his earthly life.
(f) Though, on the whole, Buddha was a rebel against priestly culture, he nevertheless shared quite a few ideas with Upanishads. Among these the most important were:
    (i) Belief in the law of *karma* and the doctrine of incarnation or rebirth.

(ii) The notion that what determines a person's next birth are the desires cherished at the time of death.
(iii) Faith in the goal of emancipation or liberation that involves transcendence of *Samsara*.
(iv) Belief in the efficacy of knowledge as the instrument *par excellence* of the attainment of *salvation*.
(v) Emphasis on internal spiritual discipline as against that on external rites and rituals accompanied by a disparaging attitude towards the sacrificial cult.
(vi) The conviction that the state of *Moksha* or *Nirvana* marks the end of the spiritual quest and the summit of spiritual attainment from where there is no falling back into the condition of *Samsara* which is necessarily fraught with suffering.

BODHISATTVA: AN IMPORTANT INGREDIENT OF BUDDHIST HUMANISM

The *Bodhisattva* is greatly moved by the spectacle of the misery of the people around him—the worldlings deluded by ignorance. They are attached to sensual pleasures and are enslaved by egotism, pride, false opinion, lust etc., and know no rest. The plight of the worldlings moves the Bodhisattva to pity and compassion. Determined to help the creatures, he reflects:

> Whatever Good I have acquired by doing all this, may I (by the merit) appease and assuage all the pains and sorrows of all living beings. . . . May I be like unto a healing drug for the sick. . . . May I allay the pain of hunger and thirst by showers of food and drink. . . . I renounce my bodies, my pleasure and my Merit in the past, present and future, so that all beings may attain the Good. . . . May I be the protector of the helpless. May I be the guide of wayfarers. May I be a boat, a bridge and a cause bay for all who wish to cross (stream). May I be a lamp for all who need a lamp. May I be a bed for all who lack a bed. May I be a slave to all who want a slave (Hardayal, 1970, pp. 57–58).

Both *Advaita* Vedanta and the *Mahayana* School of Buddhism believe in the possibility of *Jivanmukti* (liberation in lifetime) for the person who has attained right vision or the true insight into the nature of things.

The emphasis on *ahimsa* as the main constituent of righteousness or *dharma* is another important element in the Buddhist humanism. It is considered not merely as a negative measure preventing injury to creatures but also as contributing positively to their well-being *(yad ishad api paropakarkam tat sarvam apy ahimsantas samvihitam)*. Commenting on a verse in *Chatuhsataka* of Aryadeva (XII.23) Chandrakirti observes: 'that which is helpful to others in any measure, is all included within Ahimsa'.

This in short is a survey of the more important contributions toward a humanistic outlook on life to be met within the rich Indian tradition of religio-philosophic thought both ancient and modern. The importance attached to the category of *Atman* in the Upanishads and the systems of metaphysical thought deriving from them, to existential suffering in Buddhism and to the ideal of *Jivanmukti* in the entire range of spiritual reflections provide solid basis for the development of humanistic philosophy of life.

The humanistic elements found in the Indian cultural tradition, as also those present in other traditions, stand in need of redefinition and reformulation, before they can be welded into a unity of vision acceptable to the modern mind. That mind is prone to apply stricter standards of evidence or validation than those known to ancient and medieval civilizations. Thus the Upanishadic concept of *Atman* has to be replaced by the concept of man as known to us in his concrete existence, individual and social; the concept of *Jivanmukti,* too, needs redefinition or reformulation in terms of having reference to the concrete being of man-in-society. The spiritual vision of the Upanishads, their ideals of detachment and renunciation, of *nishkama karma* and *moksha* follow from their metaphysical world-view, that conceives man as *Atman* in his essential nature. The humanistic philosophy of life should likewise start with a conception of man that would enable us to impart a rational basis to the ideas and values vaguely present in modern man's consciousness.

Religion is man's response to the totality of meanings involved in the possibilities of his finite existence; it is a device to adjust to that totality in a manner that would make life bearable and possibly cheerful.

There are two broad categories of religions, the religion of faith (and worship) and the religion of knowledge and wisdom. As faith is directed on a deity it may tend to dissociate man from the affairs of the world and that of the service of man: a sense of detachment is also characteristic of the man of wisdom. But the man of faith may serve humanity if he believes that by doing so he would please his God, and the wise man, driven by his sense of compassion, may actively set about to enlighten humanity.

The two sorts of religious career are exemplified in a superlative degree in the lives of Mahatma Gandhi and Gautam Buddha. Substitute the impulse for higher and nobler life, or truth, as Gandhi calls it, for traditional godhead, and you have the humanistic religion with accent on both service of humanity and the acquisition of knowledge and wisdom. Whether a person believes in God or not, philosophic wisdom involves a measure of detachment toward purely personal concerns. Among world religions Buddhism lays greatest and most systematic emphasis on the metaphysical doctrine of egolessness and cultivation of non-egotism. This emphasis is acceptable to humanism.

Some degree of detachment toward the personal, consciously cultivated and nourished, enables a person to be impartial and just . A measure of religion or religiousness is a prerequisite of effective cultivation of the higher cultural self, consisting in the realized vision of truth and beauty. To be religious in our sense is to be lifted up and above the level of merely biophysical existence, into a region where cultivated human person enjoys a common spiritual being or existence.

It is man's capacity for detachment that prompts and enables him to build institutions providing for justice and the conditions of harmonious living. This attitude if extended to the community and ultimately to nations, the cultivation of the virtue of detachment by world leaders in economic and political fields is likely to contribute to the establishment, through the enforcement of truly just and equitable norms of conduct, harmonious relations among classes and nations.

HUMANISM AND ANCIENT INDIAN POLITY

Promotion of people's welfare

It is clearly mentioned in the following passage of *Arthashastra:*

In the happiness of his subjects lies his (the king's) happiness; in their welfare his welfare; whatever pleases him he shall not consider as good, but whatever pleases his subjects he shall consider as good.

Prajasukhe sukham rajnah prajanam ca hite hitam na-atmapriyam hitam rajnyah prajanam tu priyam hitam.

Ever was the function of promoting the welfare of the people raised to such dignity as when Kautilya compared it to the performance of a great religious sacrifice!

According to modern writers on politics, the function relating to the promotion of the general welfare of the people is only an optional one on the part of the State; while, with the ancient Indian State, the function was an essential attribute of its existence.

King Under Law

Apart from the operation of the coronation oath, the checks and limits imposed by the *paura-Janapada* and the council, there was the all-powerful Law, the common Law of the Hindu and as the king of the kings (*vyavastha-darpana*). In Manu, the king is made liable to be fined (VIII:336). It reads as follows: "Where common man would be fined one *Karshapana*, the king shall be fined one thousand; that is the settled law".

Separate Judiciary and Executive

Administration of justice under Hindu monarch remained always separate from executive, and generally independent in spirit. Proper justice was provided. Actual administration of justice is to be seen in Pali canons (*Vinaya Pitaka, Chulla vagga*: VI.4.9.). Anathapindaka vs. Jeta, the royal prince decided in the Grihapati vs. Rajkumar in the court of Sravasti, *Pradvivaka* (chief justice) and *Dharmadhikari* (Minister of law) is an example.

Dominating position of law throughout the history

Law administered by communal *sabha* (same history as court). It was not an outcome of King's household (Royal *sabha*) but of the Vedic folk-assembly. History was against a possibility of the *sabha* becoming the footstool of the throne. When it became the king's right and duty to maintain the administration of justice, he exercised it in accordance with the condition laid down and accepted through the coronation oath. He had to administer scrupulously the law of the country.

Ownership of land; not of king's but of people

The earth is not the king's but is common to all beings enjoying the fruit of their own labor. It belongs, says *Jaimini*, to all alike (*sabara* on *Jaimini*,VI.7.3):

Yavata bhogena sarvvabhaumo bhumeriste tavata anyoapi na tatra.

Madhava: 'Hence Land is not King's wealth – common wealth of all living being'

Arthasastra: "The king is the protector (*Pati*), according to the opinion of the learned *sastras,* of the *bhumi* (land) and water. Excepting these two whatever wealth there may be, his family members have sameness of right therein". Mimamsa supports this.

Raja bhumeh patirdrishtah shastragnyairudakasya cha;
tabhyamanyatra yadravyam tatra samyam kutumbinam.

The same is also supported by the Jatakas (Vol. 1, p. 398).

King constitutionally servant of the people

A king has no personal likes; it is the likes of the subjects (that should be followed by him).

Prajasukhe sukham rajnyah prajanam cha hite hitam;
Natmapriyam hitam rajnah prajanam tu priyam hitam.
Raja bhumeh patirdrishtah shastrajnairudakasya cha;
Natmapriyam hitam rajnyah prajanam tu priyam hitam.

(See: *Arthashastra*, Bk. I, Ch. 19)

CHARACTER OF HINDU MONARCHY

(a) *State: a Trust*

Shukla Yajurveda: *IX.22*: "This state to thee (is given), Thou art the director, regulator, firm bearer (of this responsibility), for (the good of) agriculture, for well-being, for prosperity, for growth (of the people), (that is) for success". This *mantra* was to be repeated at every coronation.

If the object of the trust is not fulfilled, the trustee is "to be shunned like a leaky ship on the sea (*Mahabharata: Shanti Parva: LVII.43*).

(b) *A Welfare State*

The end of the state was to secure peace and prosperity of the people. By prosperity was meant material prosperity, land, culture, wealth etc. for even in the Vedic age the king was not a priest.

(c) *A Civil State*

Militarism as a feature is everywhere absent. Paramount position is that of Law.

(d) There is no conflict between people and the Crown.

To sum up, the Hindu polity has a free career of at least three thousand years—longer than that of all the polities known to history (China is the only parallel). The test of a polity is its capacity to live and develop and its contribution to the culture and happiness of humanity. Hindu polity judged by this test will come out very successfully.

The theoretical position of polity in ancient India was based upon the concern for the people and was not anarchical. Long before the second century BC, we find mention of elective kingship and the law of nature which even kings had to obey on pain of deposition. Also, kings were required to take a pledge never to be arbitrary and always to act according to "whatever law there is and whatever is dictated by ethics and not opposed to politics" (*Aitareya Brahmana, I.14; Mahabharata: Shanti Parva: LIX,* 106–107; K.P. Jayaswal, 1955, pp. 184 and 216).

Kautilya, not only affirmed and elaborated the civil and legal rights first formulated by Manu, but also added a number of economic rights. While categorically asserting that an *arya* can never be subjected to slavery, he ordains that "the king shall provide the orphans, the aged, the infirm, the afflicted and helpless with maintenance; he shall also provide subsistence to the helpless expectant mothers and also to the children they gave birth to." (Shamashastri, 1960, pp. 47 and 206). In the ancient period, private ownership of land was not recognized. Land could not be made a private property even by a decree of the king. The above theoretical position may now be examined in the reigns of the two great rulers of the Mauryan dynasty in the 4th and 3rd centuries BC.

CHANDRAGUPTA

The *Arthashastra* clearly states that the king should look upon the people as "children for whose welfare the head of the state was responsible, and to whom he owed a debt which could only be discharged by good government".

The *Arthashastra,* further states that "When in the court, he (the king) shall never cause his petitioners to wait at the door, for when a king makes himself inaccessible to his people and entrusts his work to his immediate officers, he may be sure to engender confusion in business, and to cause thereby public disaffection, and himself a prey to his enemies. He shall, therefore, personally attend to the business of gods, of heretics, of Brahmanas learned in the Vedas, of cattle, of sacred places, of minors, the aged, the afflicted, the helpless and of women; all this in order (of enumeration) or according to the urgency or pressure of these works. All urgent calls he shall hear at once".

ASHOKA

In order to fully appreciate the humanistic approach of the rule of Ashoka we may examine some of his inscriptions:

PE IV (Delhi-topra): "Just as (a person), having made over his child to a skilful or wise nurse, feels confident (with the idea) that the skilful nurse will easily be able to protect my child. Thus, (with such an idea) my *Rajjukas* have been appointed for the welfare and happiness (of my country-people)".

yatha hi praja vyaktayai dhatrai nisrjya (janah) ashvastah bhavati-vyakta dhatri shakshyati mam prajam sukham (=sukhena) pariharttuh, evam mam rajjukah kritah janpadasya hitasukhayah.

"That there should be uniformity in judicial procedure and also uniformity in the criminal. So far too, in this matter, my rule (or injunction) is that with regard to men, who are confined to prison and later sentenced to death, after their punishment has been adjudicated (or settled in court), a grace (a respite) of three days is granted by me".

vyavahara-samata cha syat dandasamata cha. Yavat itah api cha mam ayuktih:-Bandhana-baddhanam manushyaṇamtirata-dandanam prapta vadhanam trini divasani maya yautakam dattam.

"Their relatives (during this reprieve) will make some (of the *Rajjukas*) to ponder (as a revision or review case) over the question of saving their life (i.e., by submission of an appeal for life concession). If there does not occur any such person for making them reconsider (the matter), they (the condemned persons) may (by themselves) give alms or gifts, or will observe fasts" (for benefits) in other world.

(Basak,1959, pp. 90–96)

Gyatikah va kan nidhyapayishyanti jivitaya tesham; na san va nidhyapayita, danah dasyanti, paritrikam upavasam va karishyanti.

PEV: Protection of life: (a) list of protected creatures (*avadhya*); (b) other forms of injury to living creatures was prohibited, e.g. caponing of cocks, living were not to be nourished with the living; (c) fish must not be killed, sold or eaten on specific days numbering 56 days in a year; (d) brandishing of horses and cows not permitted on certain holy days; (e) prisoners released on one day every year, probably the king's birthday.

(Mukherjee, 1942, p. 56)

PEVII: Ashoka endowed the country with a complete apparatus of public works promoting the welfare of the people: "He stood entirely for his people's welfare and progress, both material and moral." Superior officers (*mukhya*) were appointed for distribution of alms. One of the Minor PE refers to the donation of the second queen Karuvaki, mother of Tivara.

Lumbini PE: It speaks of the remission of taxes. Similarly other edicts speak of money grants (*hiranyapratividhana*) to old men and also of uniformity of punishment and procedure (*danda-samata-vyavahara-samata*) to all.

RE VI: "It is by the cultivation of these virtues (*utthan* = exertion; *arthasamtarana* = disposal of business) by utmost exertion (*parakrama*) that the king may discharge the debt he owes to his people (*anarinyam gachheyam*) in securing them (people) happiness in both this world and the next."

RE VIII: Dharmayatra instead of *viharayatra:* the program for such tours included visits (*darshana*) and gifts of gold (*hiranyapratividhan*a) to the old people who were disabled by age to work for livelihood.

RE XV:(Dhauli in Puri District of Orissa): Addressing Mahamatras stationed at Samapa, Ashoka said:

All men are my children. Just as, in regard to my own children, I desire that they may be provided with all kinds of welfare and happiness in this world and the next, the same I desire in regard to all men . . . .

(This is repeated on REXVI found at Jaugarh in Ganjam District, Orissa)

munisanam save munise paja mama atha pajaye echhami hakam (kinti davena hi) ta sukhena hidlokika-(maushyanam) sarve manushyah praja mam. Yatha prajasu ichhami aham kimiti sarvena hita sukhena Aihalaukika – palalaukikena yum (jetu ...ti tatha savamuni) esu pi ichhami hakam. (paralaukikena yunjyuh (pajah) iti, tatha sarvamanushyeshu api ichhami aham.)

Addressing *Mahamatras* of Tosali, who are also judicial officers of the city, Ashoka said: "In the administration of Justice, it sometimes happens that some persons suffer imprisonment of harsh treatment. In such cases, a person may accidentally obtain an order cancelling his imprisonment. While many other persons in the same condition continue to suffer for a long time. In such circumstance, you should so desire as to deal with all of them impartially".

Ekapulise piyathiye bandhanam va palikilesam va papunati. Tata hoti akasmaten bandhanantika anne ch bahujanedaviye dukhipati (eka purushah api ast yah bandhanah va pariklesham va prapnoti; Tatra bhavati akasmat ten Bandhanantikam, anyah cha bahujanah daviyah duhkhapate.)

From the above the following may be deduced about the judicial procedure under Ashoka:

(a) That the highest ministers called the *mahamatras* in their judicial capacity were called the *nagara-viyohataka;*
(b) That they dealt with many thousands of men;
(c) That their duty was to execute the Emperor's orders;
(d) That they were well provided for (*suvihita*);
(e) That they administered according to *niti* (*nitiyam*, i.e., *dandaniti*);
(f) That they consequently decided cases, but, in doing so, sometimes with reference to an individual and not to the larger body of litigants;
(g) That in the course of the administration of justice, a single person suffered either imprisonment or torture, while the others escaped, that is, in the course of the administration of justice, there was a chance of a single innocent man's being punished, while the many who were guilty, escaped punishment;
(h) That the judges had to be impartial;

(i) That they were not to fall victims to the many dispositions enumerated or to anger or to hurry;
(j) That they were not to be fatigued while conducting their duties;
(k) That they were implicitly to carry out the orders of the Emperor;
(l) That they were not to impose punishments involving undeserved fettering and harsh punishments; and
(m) That their work was supervised every five years by imperial superintendents of the rank of *mahamatras*, and every three years by provincial superintendents (also of the same rank) from Ujjain and Taxila, who were to see that the judicial *mahamatras* carried out the Emperor's orders to the letter.

The following humanitarian considerations are apparent in his judicial system:

(a) That the extreme penalty of death was not abolished but, like imprisonment and torture, was reduced in severity, for some time, is proved by the PE IV of Delhi-topra;
(b) Solicitude for the welfare of prisoners. Ashoka was definitely against undeserved harsh treatment and imprisonment of prisoners. He followed Kautilya in this respect whose solicitude for the welfare of prisoners is almost modern in spirit.
(c) Respite to, and release of, prisoners.

PE IV: Grant of three days respite is mentioned.
PEV proves that the king has ordered the release of prisoners on many occasions. "Until (I had been) anointed twenty-six years, in this period the release of prisoners was ordered by me twenty-five times".

Turning to the other great end of the state, social good, we may find that the concept of Ashoka approached that of Kautilya. This aspect of the question may be studied from the following points of view: Protection, medical relief, *samaja*, aid to the destitute, and *ahimsa*.

(a) Protection. The maintenance of *dharma*, which Ashoka had made the cardinal principle of his government was one of the duties of the state, while the other was that which guaranteed protection of all the subjects. *RE VI:* "And whatever effort I am making (is made) in order that I may discharge the debt (which I owe) to living beings, (that) I may make them happy in this (world), and (that) they may attain heaven in the other (world)." ". . . for I consider it my duty (to promote) the welfare of all men".

In separate *RE 1* at Jaugarh, he proclaims the following: "All men are my children. As on behalf of (my own) children I desire that they may be provided by me with complete welfare and happiness in this world and the other world, even so in my desire on behalf of all men." Cf. Kautilya: "the king is bent upon doing good to all people (*sarva bhuta hite ratah*) will enjoy the earth unopposed".

(b) Social good. The welfare of all the sections of the people (*Yogakshema*) is mentioned in Ashokan edicts. It is precisely the *hitasukham* of Kautilya. Cf. Impartiality of the judges to all sections of the people.

The second method, which aimed at social welfare, was concerning benevolent works constructed for the good of all. These consisted of planting banyan trees on the road sides, raising mango groves, digging up wells at a distance of eight *kos*, with steps for descending into the water, and numerous drinking places.

The third method by which social welfare was achieved by Ashoka refers to medicinal plants. Emperor Ashoka not only made it toll free but also imported medicinal plants from the lands of the Mediterranean Sea. Truly did the great Emperor confer one of the greatest boons on suffering humanity by this benevolent measure.

The fourth method by which Ashoka added to social good was by declaring certain items as either good or harmful to society. In RE 1 he differentiates between festivities which were permissible and those which were prohibited: "And no festival meeting (*samajas*) must be held. For king *Devenampriya Priyadarshin* sees much evil in festival meetings".

The fifth method by which social good was secured by Ashoka was by giving State aid, through the *dharma-mahamatras*, to the destitute and the sages (*anathesu vudhesu*).

The sixth method consisted in the observance of non-injury to living animals, or *ahimsa*, as we might call it in the modern days.

VEDANTA IN MODERN INDIAN THOUGHT

Hindu thought and culture received a temporary setback during the Middle Ages when Islamic conquerors established their rule over considerable areas in the Indian subcontinent. Hinduism sought to recover from the cultural shock delivered by Islam by reinterpreting its Vedantic heritage along theistic lines in the form of Navya-Nyaya in the medieval period.

In the 19th century again we see the revival of old Indian thought:

(a) Raja Rammohun Roy (1722–1833): Established Brahmo Samaj in 1828.
(b) Swamy Dayananda Saraswati (1824–83): Established Arya Samaj which preached impersonal Upanishadic Brahman or God.
(c) Debendra Nath Tagore (1817–1905) and Keshab Chandra Sen (1838-84) of Brahmo Samaj.
(d) Ramkrishna Paramhamsa (1834–86) and Swami Vivekananda (1862–1902).

As an interpreter of Vedantic Hinduism, Vivekananda has had few equals in modern times.

1. Vivekananda was a rationalist. He rejects the authority of the Vedas. He believes in the soul's union with Brahma. He praises Buddha in Karma Yoga, because he also preaches that do not believe if it does not conform to reason . . . 'then if you find that it will do good to one and all, believe it, live up to it and help others to live up to it'. ' The proof of religion depends on the truth of the constitution of man, and not on any books.
2. Another important point in Vivekananda's interpretation of Vedanta, which again is very much in line with the tradition, is his emphasis on the dignity of man. Brahman or Godhead being identical with man's essential self, God is to be sought

within one's own self. Upanishadic description of man is as "children of immortal bliss" (*amritasya putrah*), which may be seen clearly in his address:

"Ye are the children of God, the sharers of immortal bliss, holy and perfect beings. Ye divinities on earth-sinners! It is a sin to call a man so; it is a standing libel on human nature"

(Parliament of Religions: Chicago, Sept.1893)

3. An admirer of Sankara, the compassionate Buddha, the *nishkama karma* of the *Bhagavadgita*, Vivekananda was a great patriot who preached the gospel of service to weak and the needy .This was his practical Vedanta. He declares: ' The society is the greatest, where the highest truths become practical. . . .' This is almost pure humanism.
4. Vivekananda did not approve of the caste system. In his lecture entitled "Vedanta and Privilege", delivered in London, he expressed his admiration for Buddha who assailed caste-division and attempted to 'break down privilege'. Buddha preached the idea of the equality of all man. He quotes Christ as saying, "Sell all that thou hast, and give to the poor, and follow me".

Humanism alone can provide a meeting-ground in the ethics of service and love to such otherwise divergent creeds as Hinduism and Christianity.

This in short is a survey of the more important contributions toward a humanistic outlook on life to be met within the rich Indian tradition of religio-philosophic thought—ancient and modern. The importance attached to the category of *Atman* in the Upanishads and the systems of metaphysical thought deriving from them, to existential suffering in Buddhism and to the ideal of *Jivanmukti* in the entire range of spiritual reflections provide solid basis for the development of humanistic philosophy of life.

The humanistic elements found in the Indian cultural tradition, as also those present in other traditions, stand in need of redefinition and reformulation, before they can be welded into a unity of vision acceptable to the modern mind. That mind is prone to apply stricter standards of evidence or validation than those known to ancient and medieval civilizations. Thus the Upanishadic concept of *Atman* has to be replaced by the concept of man as known to us in his concrete existence, individual and social; the concept of *Jivanmukti*, too, needs redefinition or reformulation in terms of having reference to the concrete being of man-in-society. The spiritual vision of the Upanishads, their ideals of detachment and renunciation, of *nishkama karma*, and *Moksha* follow from their metaphysical world-view, that conceives man as *Atman* in his essential nature. The humanistic philosophy of life should likewise start with a conception of man that would enable us to impart a rational basis to the ideas and values vaguely present in modern man's consciousness.

THE CONCEPT OF HUMANISM IN GREECE AND THE WESTERN WORLD

Humanism is a word, which is used by writers in philosophy in many different senses. One of these implies that man makes up the entire framework of human thought, that there is no God, no superhuman Reality to which he can be related or can relate himself. But there is another tradition which defines: Humanism is a wish to find the source and the criterion of what is good, just and beautiful in the human gift, without eliminating God as irrelevant.

In the preface to his Spalding Lectures at Oxford, *Eastern Religions and Western Thought*, Radhakrishnan has said of this age: "Man has become the spectator of man. A new *humanism* is on the horizon. But this time it embraces the whole of mankind". The basic thing in our thinking should be, understanding, reconciliation, and this covers not only the relationship between human beings but also between ideas, ideals, and values. This attempt will unite rather than divide. The attempt should be to see the unity in diversity, the common factors below apparent dualism. It is not possible to find instances of un-adulterated humanistic philosophy in ancient and medieval cultural traditions, eastern or western. True humanism should be not only reluctant but also unwilling to exclude any important human concern or institution that has played a significant role in man's cultural history, from its purview. Even today religion remains a force to be reckoned with and only a few intellectuals in the West claiming to be humanist feel compelled to severe their connection from Orthodox Christianity.

The basic question facing the humanist is: can humanism find a way to preserve and defend the best in the moral and spiritual traditions of mankind without invoking supernatural authority? In order to find an answer to this question we shall have to examine the history of humanistic thought in the west.

Humanism is an attitude of mind attaching prime importance to man and human values, often regarded as the theme of Renaissance Civilization. Renaissance humanism is traceable to the fourteenth century Italian humanist, Petrarch, whose scholarship and enthusiasm for classic Latin writings ("the humanities") gave great impetus to a movement that eventually spread from Italy to all of western Europe. The universal use of Latin and the invention of movable type facilitated its diffusion. Though humanism gradually became identified with classroom studies of the classics, it more properly embraced any attitude exalting man's relationship with God, his free will, and his superiority over nature. Philosophically, *humanism made man the measure of all things.*

In its return to antiquity, humanism found inspiration in man's personal quest for truth and goodness. Confining systems of philosophy, religious dogmas, and abstract reasoning were shunned in favor of human values. Though ceaseless efforts were made to relate ancient world, seeds were likewise sown for the flowering of Reformation thought.

In recent years, the term humanism has often been used to refer to value systems that emphasize the personal worth of each individual but that do not include a belief in God. There is a certain segment of the Unitarian Universalist Association that is non-theistic and uses religious forms to promote social reform. The American Humanist Association publishes a quarterly magazine, *The Humanist*, and propagates the humanist point of view.

In addition to this non-theistic humanism, there is a tendency among Christian theologians to refer to Christianity as humanistic. Karl Barth, a noted 20th century Swiss Protestant theologian, affirmed that "there is no humanism without the

Gospel". Similarly, Roman Catholic theologians have claimed that Catholic Christianity is humanistic in that it emphasizes the uniqueness of man as being created in the image of God.

HISTORY OF HUMANISTIC SCHOLARSHIP

Scholarly efforts were made through the past two thousand years to work out and develop cultural tradition emanating from two classical focuses in the pre-Christian era: the age of Periclese in the mid-fifth century BC in Athens and that of Augustus around the birth of Christ, which eventually merged with Judo-Christian tradition to form the spiritual foundation of western civilization.

THE HUMANIST TRADITIONS

Humanism in the West derives from Greek sources and follows Greek exemplars; it is pre-Christian but there was a marriage of Christianity with Greek culture, of Hebraism with Hellenism which after the separation of the early Middle Ages was revived during the Renaissance and has survived, however loosely. This was a marriage of affinities, a marriage of two minds in heaven, not merely an arrangement of convenience forced on the parties by the circumstances of time. The thinking of Plato and Aristotle and of the Neo-Platonists and Stoics continually united with and fertilized the thinking of the Christian Fathers and of later theologians down to the end of the seventeenth century and after. When humanists think of freedom of inquiry and toleration, civil liberties and the rights of man, they think of the Church as obscurantist and oppressor and of the freethinkers as bearers of enlightenment and campaigners for emancipation, and of course this is exactly true by definition if 'freethinker' is used to denote these pioneers of enlightenment and emancipation; but was Locke, an exemplar of his age, truly a 'freethinker', or the founding fathers of the American Republic? These men and others who played a historical part in establishing freedom of inquiry and civil liberties were, most of them, religious men, though unorthodox, and did not repudiate the Christian tradition.

The peak periods of 'humanism', namely, the *Greek Enlightenment*, the Renaissance, the European Enlightenment, and its prolongation into various movements of the nineteenth century, were in great part humanist in character, were certainly not Christian, and were formative periods that transformed a dominant part of the original Europe of the Church into modern secular industrial democracies. This broad tradition, represented historically by ' The Age of Humanism' and 'The Age of Reason' and today by scientific culture in a political democracy, is broadly humanist and is definite and dominant enough to be clearly identifiable as the mainstream of Western tradition, although liable to interruption (for example, by Nazism) and exception (Spain). The 'open mind', the 'open society', and the sciences and 'humanities' are the glory of humanism and at the same time a widely shared inheritance.

Within this broad increasingly shared humanist tradition there is a strong current, an undercurrent, of humanism. The Epicureans in the classical world and the Utilitarians in the modern world best represent this inner tradition and continuity, but there are other men and movements that share this identity. As a particular school of thought or 'sect' this tradition is narrower but more clear-cut.

There are, then, two humanist traditions, a mainstream tradition which becomes dominant in Europe after the Renaissance and a minority tradition, which expressly excludes the divine, and immortal from human interests. This explicit humanism is sometimes an undercurrent that forces the pace of the flow, sometimes an underset flowing in a contrary direction. The main patterns are clearly seen in Greek thinking before the advent of Christianity.

Let us now examine in detail the evolution of the concept of humanism in the western world in different periods.

THE GREEK ENLIGHTENMENT

The developments of the Greek genius, which culminated in the Athens of Preicles in the fifth century BC, have been called the Greek Enlightenment. Homer was the most formative influence upon Hellas, as the Bible has been on some Protestant communities. This epic celebration of achievements in the Heroic

Age came to mean admiration of excellence in all human activities, in the athletic games, in the theatre, in building and sculpture, in oratory, in statesmanship, in thinking, in living. Devotion to excellence, cultivation of the highest standards in everything to which man's hand can be put is an educational ideal. Perecles called Athens 'the school of Hellas', and Hellas became the school of Rome and Europe.

The famous speech put into the mouth of Pericles by Thucydides on the occasion of the public funeral for those who had fallen in the Peloponnesian War (Chapter vi) is not strictly documentary but it does document the humanist ideal of the Athenian Greeks of that age, which is delineated in deliberate contrast to the ideal and practice of their rival city-state, Sparta. Athens is an open society; Sparta is closed and rigid, organized exclusively for war, disciplined only in martial values and virtues. Pericles gives the picture of a relaxed society, at the same time ready and able promptly to defend itself and meet all emergency requirements. The Athenians are described as versatile individualists happily engaged in their private pursuits without comments from neighbors, their city wide open to foreigners not only in trade but also in the exchange of ideas.

The idealized model of the open mind and the open society in the Periclean Athens is the main source of the broad humanist tradition. For both Matthew Arnold and John Stuart Mill, nineteenth century apostles of humanism, it was the model that represented the ideal union of culture and democracy, which they strove to establish in the modern world.

Thucydides' *History* itself is a unique humanist document, in its method and in its manner, mature and sophisticated yet fresh and graphic, charged with a sense of glory and the fatality of human affairs yet accepting human responsibility and not overborne by the worse possibilities which too often took shape. For humanist aspirations the oration of Pericles is the script, but for the whole hardy and uncertain human enterprise the *History* itself is the documentary. Hippocratic School is an unsurpassable example of the candor and equal humanity, which distinguish the humanist spirit.

Plato and Aristotle are splendid luminaries in the firmament of culture, without question. Yet in most important respects from a humanist point of view Plato is the enemy and Democritus, of whom there is some evidence that Plato was desperately jealous, is the champion.

The pre-Socratic philosophers engaged in a sustained inquiry, striving by observation and reflection to arrive at an understanding of the cosmos and of man disentangled from the traditional myth. There emerged an evolutionary view, with a main culmination in the atomic theory of Democritus, a naturalistic view, which was purely speculative but remarkably anticipated the modern scientific picture in its main features.

Protagoras of Abdera, the city from which Democritus came, was well known in Athens, a friend of Pericles, and the father of the Sophists who went from city to city giving public instructions for a fee. He was said to have introduced the so-called Socratic method of discussion. From the surviving reports and the few extant sentences of his writings, it seems certain that he was an agnostic and positivist and relativist, an acutely analytical intelligence with strong practical interests, the man who first proclaimed the *regnum hominis.*

Democritus and Plato have worked out two permanent and radically opposed views of nature and man:

(a) Nature is a non-rational order and
(b) Nature is a rational order, the product of a designing mind, and man's reason can do nothing better—and in the long run nothing other—than study and follow nature and fulfill the divine design.

These two contrary philosophies in the name of Democritus or Protagoras and Plato fully represent early in the Western tradition the most typical and deepest division in human thought and practice, still unresolved Plato's view and his totalitarian utopias, and in Neo-Platonism to an alienation from the body and from the world is absolutely an anti-humanism. Democritus, on the other hand, leads to 'the life of reason' as exemplified by Epicurus in universal terms not defined nor confined by the possibilities of a particular city, and by later humanists in different circumstances.

All the same, Plato's genius as a supreme literary artist has enriched the mainstream of humanist tradition. His creation of the charismatic teacher and sage, Socrates, has been comparable to the Gospels. Plato's thinking led to theosophy and mysticism, Aristotle's to scientific research separated from the philosophy at Alexandria.

Plato in the incomplete plan of the later Dialogues was using a cosmogony as the basis and proof of a spiritual philosophy. Aristotle shared this interest, but his program carried him away from it in the direction of disinterested empirical sciences, and his system remained provisional and open. The later, post-Socratic, schools of philosophy tended to become self-sufficient and total systems—Stoics and Epicureans. They represent the typical contrary view of nature and of man which were found before and have continued since, 'idealist' and 'materialist' or 'religious' and 'naturalist' or 'humanist'. The moral ideal for both was self-sufficiency or independence, to be master of one's fate. All men have in reason the divine spark and are equal and brothers.

Epicurus both emphasized the disparity between the divine and the human and disposed of the prevalent fear of the gods by teaching that the gods live in a remote abode of the blessed and have no interest at all in human affairs, and that man was mortal; none survived the death of the body. Thus, by wise choice and avoidance, one could keep one's fate in one's own hands securely to the end, and die full and content.

The sane influence of Epicureanism is clear in Lucian and Horace and in Montaigne and Moliere, and through these and others it has percolated down the main tradition—influencing, for example, Erasmus and More in the Christian sphere. Epicurus was the deliberate enemy of Plato whose school Cicero favored.

CLASSICAL SOURCES OF PROGRESS

Christianity was in principle irreconcilable with Greek philosophy, as faith is with reason or the human with divine. With the dominance of the Church, free inquiry was suppressed and survived only with the refugees from the Empire. In 529 Justinian closed the Academy of Athens. With the ascendancy of the Church and the decline of Rome, the elements of the humanist tradition—freedom of inquiry, political freedom, and personal independence—were dissolved. Civilization as the human enterprise was interrupted. If the classical world ended in intellectual bankruptcy and political breakdown (the 'decline and fall of Rome'), what were the achievements? The following points may be considered in this regard:

(a) Fifth century Athens remained a model of the open mind and the open society. Cicero, Plutarch, and Lucian continued to practice and to preach freedom of inquiry as a quest for a personal view of the world and way of life, down to the time when Church acquired the political power to discourage such inquiries.

(b) George Sarton (1959) is of the view that 'Modern science is the continuation and fructification of Greek science and would not exist without it'.

(c) The word 'classic' records the pre-eminent success of the Greeks and Romans in their power to awaken and educate succeeding generations by their own excellent achievements.

(d) Indeed, all the essentials of humanism in the specific sense were well understood in antiquity: the talking of all things as open to inquiry; the open city sustained by discussed and agreed cooperation sustaining independent personal lives, and as open to the exchange of ideas as of goods; in all things the pursuit of excellence informed by knowledge and techniques; separation of the divine and the human, with concentration upon the human development as an alternative to religion; rejection of absolutes and recognition of relativism as a dependable and sufficient basis of knowledge, for society, for morals; recognition of a casual and material order as a natural and firm foundation for ideals and values; acceptance of necessary conditions and limits, and cultivation of appreciation and enjoyment of what is on hand and what is in hand. Piecemeal, they found all of it; and it is all to be found there.

RENAISSANCE

The central and radial feature of the Renaissance is the work of the 'humanists'. The prototype of the humanists can be seen in the Greek sophists, The *studia humanitatis*, liberal studies, of which Cicero writes (the source of the name 'humanist') were developed out of the practical social need for letter writing and speech writing and making. The sophists taught rhetoric and practical part of philosophy, which provided practical themes of common interest for public discourse and debate. The intellectual result of this teaching has been recognized as the coming of humanism. By the fifteenth century the term *studia humanitatis*, as employed in the universities, schools, and libraries, meant a corpus of five subjects: grammar, rhetoric, poetry, history, and moral philosophy. The 'humanists' were teachers of these subjects, and also, adept in the composition of letters and speeches.

Middle Ages surely knew Virgil and Ovid, Cicero and Aristotle; but we are indebted to Renaissance humanism for the fact that we also know Lucretius and Tacitus, Homer and Sophocles, Plato and Plotinus. Though there was no basic humanist philosophy or body of thought, all the same, the humanists broadened the field of Renaissance philosophical discussion by bringing Platonism, Epicureanism, and stoicism into question as well as Aristotelianism which had been already re-established. Aristotelianism had important liberalizing effects. Aristotelianism was not only associated with the study of logic and natural philosophy in Paris and elsewhere but also in Padua with the study of medicine.

The virtue of Renaissance speculative philosophers of nature was that they sought to shake off the shackles of Greek philosophy and to find new points of departure. Francis Bacon called Telesio 'the first of the moderns', probably thinking of his empiricism and his independence from Aristotle. The celebrated, but rather shadowy, 'quarrel of the Ancients and Moderns' was thus begun.

Francis Bacon (1561–1626), in so many ways a typical Renaissance figure, is the best representative 'first of the moderns'. And Montaigne (1533–92), a generation older, writes the best epitaph on the classical verbal philosophy and the reigning theology, 'que scais-je?'. The two stands back to back, the one surveying and running over the great achievements of the past, the other analyzing the cause of failure in the progress of knowledge and proclaiming the coming and growing success by the new empirical investigation, hypothesis, and experimental test. Bacon, although completely out of touch with current scientific discoveries and inventions, was the most articulate and conscious spokesman of the 'new humanism' of the Enlightenment that was in prospect.

THE EUROPEAN ENLIGHTENMENT

Bacon's reasons, like those of Columbus, 'were afterwards made good by experience'. There was a spectacular development of human knowledge in the physical sciences in the seventeenth century. The period of 175 years between publication of *Novum Organum* and of Condorcet's *The Progress of the Human Mind* in 1795 can be thought of as the new humanism of the Enlightenment.

CONTEMPORARY HUMANISTIC VIEW OF MAN

The first view which emphasizes that man is holistic/an integrated whole, self-determining and unique, is to be seen in the *Humanistic Viewpoints in Psychology,* edited by T. Severin. The second point of view strongly supports the view that man is a holistic unity of body and personality, and concludes by pointing out that though choice, chance, and determinism are all parts of reality, man's freedom to choose can be the determining factor in how he lives and what he makes of himself (Lamont, Corliss, 1965). The third point of view distinguishes man as the user of intelligence, stresses his unique individuality, and his naturally evolved distinctive ability to be his own creator through his ideas and ideals (see: *New Views of the Nature of Man,* Edited by John R. Platt). Finally, the fourth view, is that of William James which changed five times in his own lifetime:

Stage No.	*Time Period*	*View of Man*
1.	Early 1870s and 1890s	Man is an adaptive animal
2.	Mid 1890s	Man is a moral hero
3.	Late 1890s	Man is a witness of divinity
4.	1904–1905	Man is a purely physical phenomenon
5.	1906–1910	Man is divinity

(See: Jaideep Singh (1979, p. 17)

Besides, the following five behavioral scientists who have also considered the question of humanism in the modern world are: Hubert Bonner (1965), James F.T. Bugental (1965), Erich Fromm (1947), Rollo May (1970), and Abraham H. Maslow (1953).

J. Bronowski summarizes all these five studies and comments as follows:

(a) They have consistently stressed the human search for fulfillment *within the self.*
(b) What is neglected is all that range of satisfactions which man finds in his *exploration of nature.*
(c) Behavioral scientists are indifferent to man's search to understand nature, and particularly to the *means by which man relates to external nature.*
(d) It does astonish a natural scientist that there should be no stress on knowledge as a means of human fulfillment.
(e) None of these have discussed the relation between knowledge and language—either the outer language of public communication or the inner language of discovery. There is evidence of communication between members in every species; but only in man is the outer language also transformed into an inner language for self-communication and exploration.

Bronowski says that the natural scientists with humanistic outlook have an entirely different emphasis: For example, Albert Einstein, Bertrand Russell, or Julian Huxley. Nor is this difference peculiar to modern scientists: three hundred years ago Leibnitz was already defining man in terms which stress his sympathy with the laws of nature, and philosophy of Spinoza is grounded in the same sympathy. Thus, as a natural scientist Bronowski finds it distressing, and as a humanist, he considers this attitude as a surrender to the irrational.

In his article on a 'A Twentieth Century Image of Man' he emphasizes that man, the predominantly culturally evolved animal, is distinguished by his planning and knowledge-seeking nature. Through his ability to plan man has, over the past few million years, incorporated values like affection, respect, justice, etc., into his biological nature as surely as he has created for himself a large brain.

Bronowski's definition of 'plans' is very broad, and incorporates both:

(1) Man's strategies for creating himself (values); and

(2) Man's strategies for exploring, utilizing, and creating phenomena external to himself.

Bronowski's emphasis, however, is on the latter. This is in contrast to the views of the five humanistic social scientists that have emphasized the former. According to them what distinguishes man, as a man is that he is primarily focussed on creating himself, on utilizing his powers to realize the higher human values and become the fully human person that he potentially is. As Erich Fromm summarizes it:

> While it is true that man's productiveness can create material things, work of art, and systems of thought, by *far the most important object of productiveness is man himself.* We, see, therefore, that the primary distinguishing feature of man is that he creates himself through his own choices using superrational knowledge as his chief source of guidance and energy.

According to Lamont (1965), there are ten propositions to the philosophy of Humanism:

First, humanism believes in a naturalistic metaphysics or attitude toward the Universe that considers all forms of the supernatural as myth; and that regards Nature as the totality of being as a constantly changing system of matter and energy which exists independently of any mind or consciousness.

Second, humanism, drawing especially upon the laws and facts of science, believes that man is an evolutionary product of the

Nature of which he is a part; that his mind is indivisibly conjoined with the functioning of his brain; and that as an inseparable unity of the body and personality he can have no conscious survival after death.

Third, humanism, having its ultimate faith in man, believes, that human beings possess the power or potentiality of solving their own problems, through reliance primarily upon reason and scientific method applied with courage and vision.

Fourth, humanism, in opposition to all theories of determinism, fatalism, or predestination, believes that human beings while conditioned by the past, possess genuine freedom of creative choice and action, and are, within certain objective limits, the masters of their own destiny.

Fifth, humanism believes in an ethics or morality that grounds all human values in this-earthly experiences and relationships and that holds as its highest goal the this-worldly happiness, freedom and progress—economic, cultural, and ethical—of all mankind, irrespective of nation, race, or religion.

Sixth, humanism believes that the individual attains good life by harmoniously combining personal satisfactions and continuous self-development with significant work and other activities that contribute to the welfare of the community.

Seventh, humanism believes in the widest possible development of art and awareness of beauty, including the appreciation of Nature's loveliness and splendor, so that the aesthetic experience may become a pervasive reality in the life of man.

Eighth, humanism believes in a far-reaching social program that stands for the establishment throughout the world of democracy, peace, and a high standard of living on the foundations of a flourishing economic order, both national and international.

Ninth, humanism believes in the complete social implementation of reason and scientific method, and thereby in the use of democratic procedures, including full freedom of expression and civic liberties, throughout all areas of economic, political, and cultural life.

Tenth, humanism, in accordance with scientific method, believes in the unending questioning of basic assumptions and convictions, including its own. Humanism is not a new dogma, but is a developing philosophy ever open to experimental testing, newly discovered facts, and more rigorous reasoning.

Thus, in the west, "Humanism" as a philosophy has tended to define itself in conscious opposition to theism, to the belief in (affirmation of, faith in, celebration of) a "supernatural" creator divinity. Its rather tiresome tirade against a highly simplistic straw-man interpretation of religion, its naïve embrace of science as the sole truth-telling key to nature, and its sometimes sentimental upholding of Man as the supreme value, has left many philosophers—who actually do embrace much of this position in their daily lives—embarrassed.

CHAPTER 4

Cosmogony and Cosmology

BACKGROUND

Man is by nature curious. He is always eager to know of things that come to his notice. He tries to find out the cause of every object, action, or phenomenon due to the inherent inquisitiveness of his mind. He observes imagines, argues, and learns from his experiences and draws conclusions. All our modern achievements, nay, even all that distinguishes man from other creatures, are the results of this curiosity of man. The word myth, legend, and folklore are more or less synonymous; in as much as they all signify a certain stock of traditions handed down from generation to generation. The word 'myth' primarily means a word or speech in Greek, but it has come to take on its special sense of fancy and therefore it is used for such narration or tales as are connected with gods, natural phenomena, supernatural powers, and heroes. In other words, "myths in common parlance savors of what is untrue, unreal, all the same it has a hold on man's imagination" (Macdonell, 1967, p. 1).

Cosmogony deals with the evolutionary behavior of the universe and the origin of its various characteristic features. While early cosmogonical theories were limited to the problem of the origin of our observed universe, modern cosmogony embraces the study of the origin of giant stellar galaxies, single and multiple stars, planetary systems in general, and finally the origin of atoms of various chemical elements which constitute the universe. Thus, cosmogony is concerned with the origin of the universe, whether religious, mythical or scientific, whereas cosmology is the world-view of a people, a system by which the constituent elements of their universe are related to one another. It is to be contrasted with eschatology which describes the end of the universe. Nowadays it is considered as a branch of philosophy more as a subdivision of metaphysics or as a scientific study of the origin and structure of the universe based on such things as the spectral investigation of the distribution of elements throughout the universe and the study of the redshift associated with the recession of the galaxies.

The word cosmogony is derived from the combination of two Greek terms, *kosmos* and *genesis. Kosmos* refers to the order of the universe and/or the universe as an order. *Genesis* means the coming into being or the processor substantial change in the process, a birth. Cosmogony thus has to do with myths, stories, or theories regarding the birth or creation of the universe as an order or the description of the original order of the universe. One type of narrative portraying meanings and description of creation of the universe is the cosmogonic myth. These myths, which are preserved in almost all traditional cultures, usually depict imaginative religious space and time that exist prior to the universe as a normal habitation for human beings. The beings that are the actors in this primordial time are divine, superhuman, and supernatural, for they exist prior to the order of the universe as known by the present generation of human beings.

Cosmogonic myths in their narrative form give a rhetorical, stylistic, and imaginative portrayal of the meaning of creation of the world. These myths set forth a totality and stylistics for the modes of perception, the organizing principles, and provide the basis for all creative activities in the cultural life. While these myths are always specific to the cultures in which they are found, it is possible to classify them in various ways. One may classify them according to cultural-historical strata in which they appear; thus, one might place together myths from hunter-gatherer cultures, or from early Neolithic cultures, agricultural societies, and so on. Myths may also be classified in terms of specific religion or cultural-geographical area (e.g., ancient Near Eastern, Hindu myths, etc.), or in terms of linguistic groups (e.g., Indo-European myths).

TYPES OF COSMOGONIC MYTHS

Cosmogonic myths may be classified into the following types according to their symbolic structures:

(a) Creation from nothing;
(b) From chaos;
(c) From a cosmic egg;
(d) From world parents;
(e) Through the process of emergence; and
(f) Through the agency of an earth diver.

Cosmogonic myths are seldom limited to any one of these classifications; several symbolic typological forms may be present in one myth. For example, in the *Vishnu Purana*, the creation myth shows how *Vishnu* evolves from the primordial reality of *Prakriti;* how *Vishnu* as a boar dives into the waters to bring up earth for the creation (earth diver); how creation is caused from austerities and meditation; how creation results from the churning of the primordial ocean. There is in addition the symbolism of the cosmic egg as a meaning of the creation. The classification of myths into these types is thus meant not to be a stricture of limitations but rather to emphasize a dominant motif in the myth.

Among primitive races, a cosmogony is portrayed as a single act of creation in time, with the world emerging or being shaped from one, or a few very simple, principles or elements. In Western Culture the first chapter of *Genesis* provides the best known of such creation myths and the first attempt at a philosophical cosmogony was by Thales of Miletus. But in India several millennia before him sound philosophical cosmogonical myths were narrated by the Vedic seers.

COSMOLOGY

Faced with the confusing multiplicities of nature, beyond his physical power to control, man seeks to master it symbolically by reducing it to order. Cosmology is that framework of concepts and relations which man erects, in satisfaction of some emotional or intellectual drive, for the purpose of bringing descriptive order into the world as a whole, including himself as one of its elements.

In the broadest sense of the word, cosmology is that branch of learning which treats the universe as an ordered system, and as such it is confined to a description of the salient features of the observed universe in terms of such categories as time, space, matter, etc. Cosmogony, Ontology, and Teleology are related branches of cosmology dealing respectively with the question concerning the origin, inner nature, and purpose of the universe.

It is also considered as a branch of philosophy, often considered a subdivision of *metaphysics*, that deals with the universe as a totality of phenomenon, attempting to combine metaphysical speculation and scientific evidence within a coherent framework. The problems generally falling within its province include those of space, time, eternity, necessity, change, and contingency. Its method of rational inquiry distinguishes it from purely mythic accounts of the origin and structure of the Universe.

The Pre-Socratics discussed cosmological issues, which were modified and systematized in the works of Plato and Aristotle. In the medieval philosophy, Christian theology significantly colored the whole approach to cosmology, until Renaissance science caused a radical revision of world picture. Kant maintained that the problem of cosmology was a kind that could never be solved. While some elements in cosmology have tended to be subsumed in metaphysics, others have become increasingly the concern of physical sciences.

The modern scientific study of the origin and structure of the universe is based on such things as the spectral investigation of the distribution of elements throughout the universe and the study of the redshift associated with the recession of the galaxies. Thus, it is clear that the term cosmology has double meaning: (a) the study of cosmic views in general and also for the specific view or collection of images concerning the universe held in a religion or cultural tradition; (b) a scientific study of the universe considered as a whole. It is the most encompassing task of astronomy and its distinct from, even if presupposed by, sciences with a comparatively more limited object, such as physics or geology.

For historians the study of cosmology surveys and tries to classify and understand the significance of mythical images and religious conceptions concerning the cosmos and the origin and structure of the universe. The variety of images held, historically and globally, leads to one central question: what is the relationship between man's view of the world and the validity or authority of his tradition? Hence the two meanings of cosmology do not present an ambiguity: the study of the structure of the universe and the history of the cosmological imagery are interrelated and inseparable. In contrast, the natural scientist, in his study of cosmology, does not usually need to concern himself with images of the world held in past civilizations. For the historian, however, the opposite is true: the cosmic views held by the modern scientists cannot be ignored, for they are but the latest in the long series of views and are thus worthy of consideration as those, for instance, the prehistoric Greek people and the Hindus of India.

Every aspect of a culture or religion seems to presuppose a view of the cosmos. The sacred and the phenomenon world are related, but they are by no means identical. A hierophany (a manifestation of the sacred) can lead to an image of the cosmos, but images of the cosmos do not necessarily take on a sacred significance. However, the sacred supersedes the cosmic in all religions.

Thus, it is clear that cosmology in the sense of a scientific study of the origin of the universe (which is the primary meaning of the term in modern times) cannot be the concern of a historian (as he is not competent to deal with the subject). However, as discussed above, it is very clear that the concept of cosmology in ancient civilizations is the real concern of the historians, which has all the validity to understand the world-view of the ancient people.

COSMOGONIC MYTHS OF THE INDO-EUROPEAN SPEAKING PEOPLE

The cosmogonic myths of the Indo-European speaking peoples may be varied but there are also a sufficient number of common elements to suggest the existence of an underlying Proto-Indo-European myth or myths whose general structure can be at least partially recovered. Mallory (1997, p.129) has divided creation myths of the Indo-Europeans into two broad elements—a cosmogonic myth that explains the origin of both the physical and social worlds, and a "foundation" myth that is more directly associated with the origins of mankind (anthropogonic) or the establishment of specific peoples.

Some of these cosmogonical ideograms, e.g., snake, primordial water, egg, and fish have been discussed by the author (Tripathi, 2000, pp. 1–13) where it has been discussed that all the cosmological representations available in Proto-Indo-European art of "Old-Europe" are identical to the descriptions available in the Vedic literature. Besides all these representations there is another Cosmogonic myth of the Indo-Europeans which is centered on the dismemberment of a divine being—either anthropomorphic or bovine—and the creation of the universe out of its various elements. Such myths are there in the Old Norse, Old Irish, Old Russian, Celtic, and Germanic sources. Greco-Roman traditions offer us Ovid's account of Atlas in the *Metamorphoses* (4.655–662) which relates how giant's beard and hair become forests, his bones become stone, his hands the ridges of mountains, etc. Some such myths are to be seen in the Middle Persian *Sken Gumanig Wizar* (16.8–20) of the ninth century AD. But the earliest comes from the *Purush sukta* of the *Rig-Veda* (X. 90) which describes how *Purusha*, the (primeval) 'man' was divided so that his eyes became the sun, his mouth the fire, his breath became the wind, his feet the earth, etc.

Mallory (1997, p. 130) has argued that one can discern iconographic representation of the Indo-European creation myth in the stone stelae of the early Bronze Age in the Alpine region. Here, he claims, there is a long tradition of expressing mythic concepts in stones at sites such as Val Canonic and some of the stelae, which depict a possible sunburst at the head and repeated elements such as weapons, have been interpreted, on grounds far more obvious to the proposer than others, as clear reflections of the original cosmogonic or *Purush* figure.

The cosmogonic myths, more often than not, serve as background and context for thinking about the issue of ethics. Cosmogonic myths form the horizons of meaning in cultures where they still have their original power and efficacy. Indian cosmogonic myths are particularly important for understanding myths of the Indo-European world because they have a long tradition of many a millennia (From *Rig-Veda* to *Puranas*) and are varied.

Mythology is a unique subject. It fascinates and generates interest, which remains unabated even in the face of all sorts of progress in civilization. It goes on exerting influence unnoticed on the mind of man, which leaves indelible marks on his life and thoughts. Mythology is in fact the most natural language of religion and philosophy. In India the Vedic myths and legends faithfully portray the stages of developments in religious conviction and philosophical speculations. They are the fountainhead of an extraordinarily rich cultural tradition.

VEDIC COSMOGONY

Needless to say that every culture has a 'likely story'. Given the inadequacy of discursive logic, story telling remains the only alternative to articulate what is basically inarticulable. The retelling of the likely story renews people's link with the Beyond and helps them maintain openness of their soul to the experiences of the Beyond. Only on this basis a culture succeeds in renewing and revitalizing itself. However, the likely story of creation differs from culture to culture. The Vedic civilization, too, has a 'likely story' of creation,, a story described as *shrishti vidya*, knowledge pertaining to creation, a *bhavavritta*. This story has, however, not been given proper attention for three vital reasons. First, the Vedic perspective on creation is expressed through mythopoesis, through hymns that appear unrelated, discrete, nothing more than occasional outbursts of poetic imagination; they do not seem to present a cogent, logical, and systematic account of either the creator or of creation. Apparently lacking logical consistency, Vedic hymns cast in the form of mythopoesis become suspect as a vehicle of understanding.

Second, Vedic hymns are like beautiful maidens who do not reveal their body to anyone else than their lovers (RV.X.71.4). This concealment has been possible through the use of symbols on a large scale. Its lack of confidence in language of concepts, the hallmark of logical thinking, has created an intellectual environment in which *shristi vidya* has generally been variously and, at times, vacuously interpreted spreading confusion and not infrequently calumny. And, lastly, for those under the sway of Western philosophical tradition, the Vedic *bhavavritta* is simply the unrelated outpourings of primitive mind even though, as Max Muller concedes, they constitute the first ever articulation of religious thinking. Moreover, for the West, the history of philosophical thinking does not go beyond what Carl Jasper calls the "axis time", roughly around the fifth century BC, when an unprecedented spiritual awakening took place around the world. In Israel, Greece, China, India, this awakening offered new insights and lent a new spiritual depth to thinking about the structure of order. But for all practical purposes, the beginning of philosophy and philosophy of history is traced to Judaism and Plato than to developments in China and India. As such, the real dividing line between pre-philosophic and philosophic thinking being this axis time, any development before this demarcation line is *ipso facto* treated as non-philosophic and, therefore, not worthy of consideration.

But for all this, however, the Vedic *shristi vidya* offers a very rich form of cosmological thinking as compared to cosmogonical stories prevalent in other cultures. Needless to say, the process of the One becoming the Many is the process of creation. In this connection, certain questions need to be satisfactorily answered. For instance, what does the term "creation" signify? What are the elements that go into the making of the cosmos? In speaking about cosmos one must take into account the elements that do, in fact, or promise to, maintain order. One must therefore ask: What are these elements? Are they engendered in the process of creation itself that help maintain order at the macro-cosmic plane and keep alive the possibility of gaining or regaining order in the human world?

The source of the maker of this Universe is universally acclaimed to be an entity that is all pervasive but *avyaya* (inexhaustible), *anirukta* (inexplicable or undeclared), *aparimita* (immeasurable, *apeiron* in Gk.), etc. The process of creation begins when *apeiron*, as Plato puts it, is bounded by *peras* (limits). The process of the One turning into the Many raises four interrelated questions. First, what is the nature of this Boundless? Second, what is the process through which the One turns into the Many? Third, does the One exhaust itself fully by turning into the Many? And, lastly, if the whole process of creation is unsighted even though occurring every moment before or beyond our eyes, what could be the most likely account of creation that can be rendered?

The Boundless, the *avyaya*, Idea (*Eidos*) to use the Platonic term, assumes many names (*nama*) and forms (*rupa*) and becomes embodied idea (*enhylon eidos*). This can happen in two alternate ways. First, the Boundless is a creator who makes use of materials that are already available but only in an incompletely fashioned form for creating this universe himself standing outside it; he is a demiurge or a *deus ex machima*. Alternatively, the creator is not outside this creation; the Boundless is the one substance which transforms himself into many modes of being. These many modes constituting the universe are considered to be either a *parinama* (transformation) or a *vivarta* (transfiguration) of the One. In either case, the One pervades the universe.

The One pervades the universe, to be sure. But does it exhaust itself fully in the universe it creates? If it were to do so, the universe confusedly would become God with no room left for him. In contradistinction to this, God does create the world but does not fully exhaust himself. As a matter of fact, in the Vedic cosmogony, the *Brahman*, the creator of this universe, is supposed to be *chatushpad* (having four legs); only one of his legs manifests as this universe, the *idam sarvam*, or *tode ti.* This *idam sarvam* does not fully reveal what is beyond it. That is why the Vedic seers treat the sensible world only as *praketa,* the sign of *apraketa,* of what is beyond our senses, the unmanifest reality, that is a visible symbol, or *eikon,* to use a Platonic term, of what is invisible. But what is a symbol is both like and unlike what it stands for. Apart from signifying something else, something other than what they substantively, in and by themselves, are, symbols also refer to something which they in reality are not.

Speculations about the origin of the universe started not from the *terra incognita* of the hypothetical First Principle, but from the tangible and knowable concrete. The problem of the origin of things naturally fascinated 'the brooding mind of India' in different ages as a result of which widely differing ideas centering round the cosmological problem came into existence. But one thing, which should be taken into account in this connection, is that, like all other countries of the ancient world, here also we find a process in the evolution of ideas. Ancient Indian cosmogonies may be divided into *three* categories: those beginning with the material principles like water, earth, fire, ether, etc.; those beginning with the abstract principles like chaos, time, night, desire, non-being, etc.; and those beginning with the divine principles *like Prajapati, Brahman, Vishvakarman*, etc. This holds good in the cosmogonical speculations of other countries also. Of these three categories, the first is probably the most primitive. It appears that the conception of a divine principle as the creator of the universe marks the latest stage in the development of cosmogonic ideas, though not in all cases.

It seems perfectly reasonable to the primitive peoples who saw land growing from the accumulations of river-borne silt and desert wastes rendered cultivable by irrigation, to conclude, for instance, that water was the primary element and the source of all that existed. In the famous creation hymn of the *Rigveda* (X.129) the question is raised whether the fathomless waters existed before the formation of the world and the answer is given in the affirmative. The conception of the *cosmic ocean* recurs in other mythologies as well, notably in some Greek cosmogonies and in the Egyptian and Babylonian legends of creation. Among the Greeks a number of cosmogonies were devised, the prime component of the universe being ocean according to Homer; water and earth, according to Athenagoras; and water, according to Thales (Gomperz, T.: 1901, pp. 56ff). The ancient Egyptians believed that at the beginning of the world was a waste of water called Nu or Nun, and it was the abode of the great father (Erman, A.: 1907, pp. 26ff). In Babylonian mythology, both Apsu and Tiamat were forms of water, the former representing the orderly framework of nature, the water of the annual inundation, which irrigated the Babylonian plain. The latter represented the destructive and anarchic aspects and was mythologically pictured as a dragon who was slain by Merodach or Marduk. In the later Babylonian mythology attempt was made to reconcile the antagonism between the conceptions of this watery element by making Apsu and Tiamat complementary principles. It should be pointed out in this connection that Taimata or Tiamat, the water-dragon whom the Babylonian Indra vanquishes, actually figures in the *Atharvaveda* (V.13.3), spontaneously enlightening transition from *praketa to apraketa.*

VARIETY OF COSMOGONICAL SPECULATIONS IN ANCIENT INDIA

In ancient India we come across a variety of cosmogonical speculations. As each school of thought faced the cosmogonical problems in its own way, they became very controversial. There was, for example, the major question whether the physical universe is real. In the history of Indian philosophy we come across two extreme views on this subject, represented by the materialistic school on the one hand and the *Advaita Vedanta* on the other. The former holds that the world is a spontaneous growth promoted by the combination of material elements while, according to the latter, the physical world has only an illusory reality produced by the false projection of *Maya*. But nowhere in the Vedic literature is there any ground for the suspicion that the world is to be thought of as illusion. The major Upanishads proclaim the reality of the world. We are told, prior to the creation, the world was in non-manifested form. The Samkhya-Yoga believes that the unmanifested Prakriti is real. The visible world is thought of as the product of five gross elements, viz. earth, water, fire, air, and ether. All schools of Indian thought share this view. Even in the *Advaita Vedanta* we come across the theory of *Panchikarana,* according to which the five elements mix in different proportions to produce the *Bhutas.*

The *Rigveda* postulates only water as the primordial element or matter from which others gradually evolved. In the post-vedic literature, however, the elements are said to come out from an ultimate material cause, *Prakriti* or *Maya*, through a process of evolution. In the earlier elemental cosmogonies what was demanded in the first cause was the ability to produce the effect, like water hardening itself into the earth. The changing world was taken into account by different schools of thought from their own angle of vision, and throughout the ages various views have been advanced on this problem. Some thinkers believe in some sort of positive cause behind the growth of the world and the transformation of its objects while others do not. According to one theory, the effect is practically identical with the cause while, according to another, there is absolute difference between a cause and its effect, the latter being entirely a new and fresh production. In between these extremes there are a number of theories.

In the Vedic literature we come across a kind of progress from crude and unconnected notions to more refined ideas and broader views. There was a steady but multifarious advance from a concrete physical cause to the abstract, ritualistic, theistic, physiological, and psychological first principles. It is mentioned in the *Svetasvatara Upanishad* (1.2) that Time, Nature, Necessity, or Fate is the basic cause of creation. Different thinkers have regarded chance or coincidence, elements, purusha, and combination of these at different times as the cause of the world. But the question which came into prominence ultimately were concerned with the nature of the cause itself: whether the effect is produced out of something positive or eternal or out of mere void, whether the cause alone is real and eternal and the effect merely an illusion. Philosophically to define a *cause* is a matter of proverbial difficulty, but the best idea is probably that of *producing*, wherein something real passes from the efficient cause into the entity of the effect.

But God as the efficient cause has, in fact, no part to play in the development of Indian cosmogonical ideas. In the Vedic literature the idea of an omnipotent God creating world out of his own nature without any pre-existing substance is practically absent. The main current of the Upanishadic thought flows towards a monistic conception. There is one without second.

Nothing can be positively postulated about him. Badarayana, the author of the *Vedanta Sutra,* believes that the power of creation belongs to the pure, stainless Brahman, the material and efficient cause, who for his own sport develops himself into the world without undergoing the least change. But unless Brahman as the material and efficient cause transforms himself into the world, creation cannot take place. And if he does so, he ceases to be Brahman. The eternal and infinite Brahman cannot be subject to change. In other words, the changing and impermanent world cannot be the effect of an eternal and changeless cause. Nor can the world be traced to *Prakriti* or *Maya* which is unintelligent. Therefore, in order to explain the creation of the world it is necessary to posit *Maya* or *Prakriti* by the side of the Brahman, as has been done by Sankara. But to do so, is to limit the nature of Brahman which has no second. But if no second is posited, the explanation of the world becomes impossible. Thus, as the only way out, the *Saguna* or changing Brahman is conceived who, as the Demiurgic, combines within himself both the unattached Brahman and the unconscious *Prakriti* or *Maya*. But this *Isvara* also is not real, like the worlds, because of his finite existence.

Another theistic line of argument has been offered by the later *Nyaya-Vaisesikas.* According to them, the world has the atoms for its material cause and God for its efficient cause. The atoms can act only when, prior to the beginning of creation, they are controlled by an intelligent being. God creates the world for the sake of making the beings experience the fruits of the actions of their past lives. The creation and the destruction of the world follow one another in regular order. The periodic dissolution is brought about by God's desire to reabsorb the whole creation within himself. The *Nyaya-Vaisesika* arguments have been challenged not only by the *Mimamsakas* but also by the Buddhist and Jain writers. The early *Mimamsakas* are silent about the question of God and the latter one rejects the proofs of God. According to the *Mimamsakas*, perception, inference, and scriptures do not prove God. God cannot act as the supervisor of *dharma and adharma* since he cannot have any knowledge of them. The world having neither beginning nor end does not require any creator. So far as the theistic cosmogonies of different religious sects are concerned, this much we can say that, their propounders were not at all troubled regarding the questions of how the world of imperfection could take its birth from Brahman, the absolute perfection, since they were willing to accept on the authority of *Sruti* that the finite might spring from infinite.

COSMOGONICAL AND COSMOLOGICAL IMAGES OF OLD EUROPEAN CIVILIZATION

Marija Gimbutas (1970) who used the term Proto-Indo-European Culture for the Kurgan Culture during the Fifth, Fourth and the Third millennia BC has given a chronological table of the cultural complexes of the Central and Eastern Europe (1974) during this period. I am using the term in the same sense and accepting the dates given by her. Gimbutas (1974, pp. 89 ff.) has described in detail various conventionalized and abstract ideograms, recurring on figurines, stamp seals, dishes, cult vessels, and as part of the pictorial decoration of vases and house walls which explain the cosmogony and cosmology of the people of that period as well the functions of the deities it sustained. She has divided the symbols into two basic categories: those related to water or rain, the snake and the bird; and those associated with the moon, the vegetal life-cycle, the rotation of seasons, the birth and growth essential to the perpetuation of life. The first category, according to her, consists of meanders, and spirals. The second group includes the cross, the encircled cross, and more complex derivations of the basic motif, which symbolically connects the Four Corners of the world, the crescent, horn, caterpillar, egg, and fish.

VEDIC TEXTS AND PROTO-INDO-EUROPEAN ARCHAEOLOGY

More than 30,000 miniature sculptures of clay, marble, bone, copper, and gold from some 3000 sites of the Neolithic and Chalcolithic era in South Eastern Europe along with enormous models of temples and actual temples have been reported in recent years. Marija Gimbutas (1974) has identified various cosmogonical and cosmological images of moon, bull, snake, fish, and primordial egg in them. These archaeological images are well dated on the basis of the radiocarbon analysis and their calibration with dendrochronology in c. 6500 to 3500 BC.

The cosmogonical and cosmological images could be better explained and appreciated on the basis of the study of Vedic literature and Puranas which have a long tradition. Much has been written on the date of various works of the Vedic literature. While some scholars have attached a label of high antiquity to them, others have placed them not much farther from the historical period of written records. H. Jacobi (in Winternitz, 1972, pp. 294–300) and Shankar Balakrishna Dixit (1969) have fixed the date of the *Satapatha Brahmana* in 3000 BC on the basis of the astrological calculation of a verse in it.

athaita eva bhuystha yat krittikah tadbhumneva etadupaiti, tasmat krittikaswadadhiti.

Eta ha vai prachyai disho na chyavante, sarvani ha va anyani nakshatrani prachyai dishashchyavantae (SB 2.1.2.3)

Winternitz (1972, part 1, pp. 294–300)) too agreed with them when he placed the beginning of the Brahman tradition in 2000 or 3000 BC. On the basis of the date of the Brahmanas the date of *Samhitas* may be placed in the tenth to sixth millenium BC.

I would like to mention here that some of the well-dated proto-Indo-European images of southeastern Europe are really the material manifestations of the Vedic mythological concepts and legendary ideographs. None will doubt the fact that the Vedic literature is the first written record of the human race consisting of the best thinking regarding the origin of universe, religion, and philosophy carrying traditions of thousands of years.

The exact parallels of the Vedic legendary concepts are found in these archaeological records and, as such, it would not be incorrect to place the beginnings of the Vedic tradition in the sixth millennium BC rather than in the third millennium BC. The following parallels drawn from the Proto-Indo-European art motifs, the Vedic ideograms and mythological concepts will certainly justify such an assumption.

Primeval Water

Stories regarding the creation of the universe found in the Indo-European and non-Indo-European mythologies represent stages of a long process of development. Because of their primeval character they are considered to be very old. Ethnological parallels from the fishing and hunting societies indirectly prove the palaeolithic origin of the cosmological ideas centering on water, water bird, egg, etc. During the Neolithic and the following Chalcolithic periods, stories of creation became quite complex as are seen in the vase paintings and frescoes of these periods. The primeval elements of the universe were conceived as water. The abstract paintings on Cucuteni vases from Sipintsi, Western Ukraine (mid-fourth millennium BC) reveals the formation of the world (Gimbutas, 1974, p. 99, fig. 51).

A number of cosmogonic references of the Vedic literature and the legends regarding the 'Primeval Waters' (The Flood Legend) are well known from the Brahmana literature. The water is identified with breath (*Pranah*). All gods and water are also identified with 'Amrita' which is the life-giving element. According to the *Taittiriya Samhita*, too, there was nothing but the waters in the beginning over which Prajapati floated on a lotus leaf (*Taittiriya Samhita*, 5.6.4.2.: *apo va edam asanna salilameva sa parajapatih. Pushkar parni vatoalilayate*). This idea is quite compatible with that expressed in the *Puranas*. In the Puranas *Narayana* and *Vishnu* are described as lying on the ocean of waters. They also describe waters as *'Ekarnava-Nidhi'* or *'Yugantara Toya'* (see: *Rigveda* X.190.1: *tatah samudro arnavah*; cf. *Yajurveda* 26.63; *Ramayana (Yuddha)* 104.23; *Mahabharata (Bhishma Parva)* 1.24; *Vayu Purana* 7.57-58 *ekarnave bhavantyapoh)*. These ideas of creation of the universe from water have their roots in the Vedic mythology and this ideogram is quite parallel to the art motifs of southeastern Europe dated in the fourth millennium BC.

Primordial Egg

In one of the abstract vase paintings of Cucuteni (Gimbutas, 1974, pp. 103, 124, figs. 57 and 84) the idea of the formation of the world and the beginning of life from egg, in the midst of which a germ resided, is quite clear. In the painting a plant within an egg is painted over the vase. The egg is enveloped in water shown by encircled lines. The snake winds across or around the cosmic egg. The idea of a primordial egg or vulva is likewise expressed in sculptures such as the Lepenski Vir (Northern Yugoslavia) stone sculpture in the shape of an egg with an engraved vulva design dating around 6000 BC (Gimbutas, 1974, p. 103, fig. 68).

In the Vedic cosmogony the creation of the universe is said to have taken place from the '*Hiranyagarbha*' or the 'Golden Egg'. Mahidhar explains the concept of '*Hiranyagarbha*' as *Prajapati* existing in the embryo of Brahma in the form of an egg which was golden in color from which a male (*Praja*) sprang into being before all living creatures came into existence. 'Prajapati' is 'Hiranyagarbha' says the *Satapatha Brahmana* (10.1.4.9): *tasmadahu hiranyamayah prajapatih iti, rupameva taat prajapatih hirnyamayah tat atmanokuruta;* (see also, *Rigveda* 10.121.1; *Taittiriya Samhita:* 5.5.1.2) and we have seen in the legend already discussed that the mundane egg forms an important stage in the cosmogony of the Brahmanas. *Hiranya*, i.e., the pulsating life of the impregnated egg is called the seed of Agni who meditated upon water and, united with them, cast seed into them. *Satapatha Brahmana* says that *Prajapati* completed the span of one year in this form and then stood up and broke open the golden egg. This narration is enough to prove that the Proto-Indo-European images and Vedic ideograms are quite compatible with each other in form, concept as well as in date.

The Snake

The snake and its abstracted derivatives, the spiral, are the dominant motifs of the art of old Europe throughout the Neolithic and Chalcolithic periods until the Minoan civilization, the sole inheritor of the Old European culture. The Chalcolithic Butmir, Cucuteni, and East Balkan peoples created large bulbous vessels, adopting the snake form. Spiral was the basic ornamental compositions of this period. This art motif reaches its peak in the form of unified symbolic and aesthetic expressions in 5000 BC. A coiled pottery snake decorated with incised zigzag and punctuated design was found at the early Vinca settlement of Predionica. A snake coil covers the entire inner surface of a ritual dish with holes from Kukeva Mogila in Bulgaria (Gimbutas, 1974, p. 96, figs. 54–55).

A formidable horned-snake modeled in relief winds around a Neolithic pot from the site of Suvedol-Dibel in Pelagonia. Snake, their bodies marked by dots or comb-like stamps, have been found incised on a number of vases from the Vinca mound. Snake motifs of potporang at Vrsnic yielded curling snakes (Gimbutas, 1974, pp. 94, 96, figs. 54–55).

The snake was consequently mythologized, attributed with a power that can move the entire cosmos; can make the world roll with the energy of their spiraling bodies. Snakes and plant motifs sometimes symbolize the belt of the earth. The organization of the motifs thus demonstrates that the imagery is genuinely cosmogenic.

Parallels to the Indo-European snake motifs in the Neolithic-Chalcolithic periods may be seen in the Vedic ideograms. In the *Rigveda* II.7.6 (*sarpiyasutiryasya sah agnih)* snake is symbolized as fire which is a generative element. At several places in the *Aitareya Brahmana* (5.2.3: *iyam prithivi vai sarpa rajni;* see also *Taittiriya Brahmana* 2.2.6.2.: *deva vai sarpah tesham iyam rajni*) the earth has been described as 'snake-queen'. The *Satapatha Brahmana* (7.4.1.25: *ime vai lokah sarpah tesham iyam rajni*) clearly states that the universe is like a snake and that the whole universe rolls with the earth. *Maitrayani Samhita* (2.7.201-3) describes the whole universe as an abode of snakes in different forms which clearly demonstrates the cosmogonical nature of the snakes.

Namo asta sarpebhyo ye ke cha prithivi manu,
Ye antarikshe ye divi tebhyah sarvebhyo namah.
Ye ishavo yatudhananam ye vanaspatinam'
Yeavareshu sherate tebhyah sarvebhyoh namah.
Ye ami rochane divo ye va suryasya rashmishu,
Ye apsu shadansi chakrire tebhyah sarvebhyo namah.

According to the *Taittiriya Samhita* (3.1.1.1.) in one of His creations 'Prajapati' created the snakes first and then the birds; but according to *Jaiminiya Brahmana* (2.228) he created firstly the snakes and then the fish and thereafter the birds. Thus, the above Vedic references clearly demonstrate the cosmogonic nature of snakes.

The Fish

The usual symbolism connected with the fish ranges from its being an emblem of the vulva, or the phallus, to a symbol of the soul or the 'mystic ship of life'. By microscopic analysis of engravings on Megdalenian bone objects, Mashak (1972, pp. 169 ff.) has recently shown that fish (salmon) and snake typically appear in the context of a seasonal manifestation representative of early spring and frequently in association with new shoots, young animals, and ibexes. The fish is also inseparable from the form of a phallus since the phallus offers a visual and kinesthetic comparison with the fish and snake (cf. a baton head from Gorge d' Enfer in Dordogne). An engraving in the Magdalenian cave of Lortet shows fish nuzzling a reindeer's genitals (Henze, 1932, p. 113). Many years later, in Greek Geometric art, the fish continued to be portrayed hanging on the genitals of horses; the fish is also placed with the womb of the Bee Goddess painted on a Beotian vase around 700 BC (Gimbutas, 1974, pp 84, 110, fig. 141). Its role there must have been related to the shape of a bee and is associated with the head of a sacrificial bull.

In the Neolithic art the fish assumes the shape of an egg and is anthropomorphized. This is exemplified by the sculptures recently discovered at Lepenski Vir near the Iron Gates in northern Yugoslavia (Srejovic, 1972). There, in the late seventh and early sixth millennium BC, fishing and hunting peoples had dug their houses into the bank of the Danube, houses which had trapezoidal floor plans provided with rectangular hearths sunk below the floor level, lined with stones, and outlined with thin slabs of stone set vertically in a pattern of continuous triangles. Large stone sculptures were placed in the lime-plaster floors in front of the hearths. Fifty-four of these monumental sculptures, most of them twice as large as human head, were found, and fifteen of them reveal half-human and half-fish features. Geometric ornaments are pecked on many of them while others are plain. All appear to possess aspects of either the human figures, the fish, or the egg, and were probably selected for this reason. The shape of the river boulder had a significance of its own; the artist did not alter this, but only gave it the features of the mythical being he venerated. He added the mouth and large round eyes of a fish and the nose and eyebrows of a man. The mouth with downward-drooping corners makes the facial features stern, even dramatically tense, but it is doubtful whether the painful grimace was really what the Lepenski Vir artist sought to portray; the sternness results from a peculiar combination of fish and human features and does not necessarily reflect the artist's conscious intent (Gimbutas, 1974, pp. 108–109, figs. 72–76). In his book on Lepenski Vir, D. Srejovic calls one of the egg-shaped and fish-shaped sculptures 'Danubius'. The name implies a male river divinity, but does the sculpture really represent a male and awe-inspiring god?

Geometric motifs engraved on stone sculptures, such as zig-zags, interconnected lozenges each with a dot in it, chevrons and labyrinthine designs on round stones with depressions (probably used for sacrifice) are related to the symbolism which appears as aquatic divinities associated with cosmogonical imagery. The Lepenski Vir statuary seems to represent the divinity of a feminine gender. One of the sculptures reproduced here has female breasts which incorporates aspects of an egg, a fish, and a woman. Marija Gimbutas thinks that she could have been a primeval creator or a mythical ancestress (Gimbutas, 1974, pp. 110, fig. 75). Standing at the hearth she was probably a guardian of the house also. These monumental sculptures have been found only in the Iron Gates region of Danube, and they may well be specifically connected with the cult practices of a people whose main concern and subsistence was fishing. Fish effigies, however, have been found elsewhere in the Neolithic sites where farming activities were evident. Even in the flourishing civilization of Vinca the fish must have played a part of mythical imagery, since some cult vessels were formed in the shape of a fish (Gimbutas, 1974, fig. 74).

The Indo-European fish seems to be the material manifestation of fishes in the Vedic literature in specific contexts. *Rigveda* (X.68.8) describes fish as a water species and *Taittiriya Samhita* and *Jaiminiya Brahmana* (2.228) clearly states that 'Prajapati' created serpentiles (Snake-fish) firstly.

The *Shatpatha Brahmana* (1.8.1.1-2) describes in detail how a fish preserved the seeds of species and saved Manu Prajapati for creation after the Great Flood (*manave ha vai pratah... matsyah... Audya imah sarva prajah nivvrydah tatassvaparayitasmi iti*). The incarnation theory of *Puranas* also followed the theory of 'Great Flood' and mythologies concerning it as narrated in the Vedic literature. According to the Puranas when the Flood receded Brahma (Prajapati) got incarnated in the form of a fish (*Matsyavatara*) in the deep sea (Agrawal, 1963). According to R.C. Dixitar (1935, p.14), the mythology of the 'Great Flood' found in the Hebrew, the Babylonian, and the Sumerian literature has its roots in the Vedic mythology. This story in different forms is repeated in the *Purana* and the Epics (*Mahabharata: Bhishma Parva*: 1.24; *Karna Parva*, 95.5; *Matsya Purana*, 2.3.) In the *Avesta* also we get the narration of the 'Great Flood' in a different form (*Vendidad*-2). Thus, it is clear that the association of fish with the creation of the universe is not only attested by the archaeological findings of the South-Eastern European countries in the proto-Indo-European and Indo-European contexts but also in the Vedic and other Indo-Iranian literary texts.

CONCLUSION

On the basis of a detailed study of the representation of Primeval Water, Primordial Egg, Snake, and Fish in the Proto-Indo-European and Indo-European art forms of c. 7000 BC to 4000 BC, Marija Gimbutas has rightly concluded that these representations are definitely associated with the cosmological myths of the Indo-European people. The parallels drawn from the Vedic literature and *Avesta* regarding the creation of the universe simply confirm the cosmogonic and cosmological associations of the above art motifs in the Indo-European contexts. A further study of the animals, plants and trees, both in the Indo-European art and the Vedic literature, reconfirms the above parallelisms. It would, therefore, be not a mere fancy to conclude that the antiquity of the Vedas would go further in the past. Since no artistic representations similar to those found in the Old Europe of seventh and fifth millennium BC are available in India, the Vedic cosmogony and cosmology could not be archaeologically attested. But, in the light of the proto-Indo-European and Indo-European art representations discussed above it would not be unfair to rethink about the antiquity and geographical expanse of the Vedic literature.

GREEK COSMOGONY AND COSMOLOGY

Since the word 'cosmogony' describes the origin of the universe by the figure of birth, it suggests to us in the first instance accounts of a mainly poetic and mythological kind. Yet science has its fairy tales, and one who seeks information about Greek cosmogonies might not unreasonably look for some account of that, for example, which is contained in the *Timaeus.* Hastings (1959, Vol. 4, p. 145) has divided it into (a) *poetic* cosmogonies, and (b) *philosophical* ones. Under the poetical cosmogonies he has discussed (1) Homer, (2) oldest Orphic cosmogony, (3) Hesiod, (4) Pherecydes, (5) later Orphic cosmogonies, and (6) Aristophanes. Under the philosophical cosmogonies he has discussed (1) early Ionian philosophers, (2) Empedocles, (3) Plato, (4) Aristotle, (5) Stoic cosmogony, and the neo-Platonic cosmogony.

The word *cosmos* means "order" in general, whether of the world or a household, of a commonwealth or a life. Thus when applied to the universe and becoming assigned to it as to its eminent instance, 'the word does not merely signify the neutral fact of all-that-is, a quantitative sum (as the term "the All" does) but expresses a specific and to the Greek mind an ennobling quality of this whole: that is order' (Hans Jonas, 1963, p. 241). Although the word "the cosmos" could denote only the universe, it yet never came to monopolize the meaning of the word and to oust other uses.

But more than merely the widest instance, the universe was considered to be the perfect exemplar of order, and at the same time of all order in particular, which only in degrees can approximate that of the whole. Again, since the sensible aspect of order is beauty, its inner principal reason, the All as perfect order must be both beautiful and rational to the highest degree. Indeed this bounded physical universe denoted by the name "cosmos" was considered a divine entity and often called outright a god, finally even the God. Plato, though not regarding the cosmos as the highest being itself, called it the highest sensible being, "a god", and "in very truth a living creature with soul and reason" (*Timaeus* 30B:34A). It is superior to man, who is not even the best being within the world; the heavenly bodies are his betters, both in substance and in the purity of steadiness of the intelligence that activates their motivation.

Stoic monism led to a complete identification of the cosmic and the divine, of the universe and God. Cicero, in the second book of "The Nature of the Gods", gives eloquent expression to this theological status of the visible universe. His argument, compounded of elements from Stoic sources, is supremely instructive. Man himself, however, was born to contemplate on the cosmos and to imitate it; he is far from being perfect, but he is a little part of the perfect. It establishes the connection between cosmology and ethics, between the apotheosis of the universe and the ideal of human perfection; man's task is the theoretical one of contemplating and the practical one of "imitating" the universe. Man's relation to the cosmos is a special case of part–whole relationship, which is so fundamental a theme in classical thought. It was the *cosmos* that was declared to be the great "city of gods and men," and to be a citizen of the universe, a *cosmopolites*, was now considered to be the goal by which otherwise isolated man could set his course. He was asked to identify himself with that cause directly, across all intermediaries, and to relate his inner self, his *logos*, to the *logos* of the whole.

(a) Poetic Cosmogonies

We do not find in Homer a complete cosmogony, but ideas of a cosmogonical kind, or, rather, of a geogonical, as all he is concerned about is the world in which we live in. In *Illiad (xiv, 246)* Oceanus is the father *(genesis)* of all the gods, and in xiv. 201 Tethys (*tithy*= 'nurse') is the mother. Tethys symbolizes the suckling mother, earth. But behind these Nature-powers stands a third still more august power, the goddess Night whom even Zeus fears. Lucas, therefore, thinks that for Homer Night was the supreme geogonical conception.

Orpheus made his beginning with Night. John Lydus (6th c. AD) stated that Orpheus' three first principles were: Night, Earth, and Heaven. Plato quotes a couplet from Orpheus, describing Oceanus and Tethys as the first wedded pair, while he informs us in the *Timaeus* (41 A) that Oceanus and Tethys were the off-springs of Earth and Heaven. In this Orphic cosmogony Oceanus and Tethys are a degree less venerable than in Homer; Earth and Heaven are the oldest pair. Here also, as in Homer, Night is the supreme conception. The cosmogony in Homer seems to have been borrowed from the Orphic.

Hesiod, in the introduction to his *Theogony* (verses 106–107) actually names Earth, Heaven, and Night—the reputed Orphic trinity—as the sources of the gods. Besides this, he also gives (verses 116–136) his own cosmogony. He says that in the beginning there was chaos, after whom, on the one hand, came Gaia and Eros, and, on the other, Erebus and Night. Erebus and Night were the parents of Aether (or light) and Day. Gaia of herself, first Uranus (Heaven), that he might be a cover to her round about, and that she might be a secure dwelling-place for the gods; and after him the mountains and seas. Lastly mating with Uranus, she became mother of all the gods, except the few who sprang from Erebus and Night.

On top, then, of Hesiod's cosmogony stands Chaos. It has been variously taken for Water, Air, Fire, and Space. Etymology has been appealed to in each case. However, the most probable meaning of the term seems to be Space (Gk. *xaino*= '*to gape*'). Space was Hesiod's first principle which he has pictured 'as an immeasurable, waste, and formless mass', while Lukas understands by it the mere unlimited void.

Of the next cosmogonical stage we have two pairs, of which the first is Gaia and Eros. Gaia is the Earth, not however as an element, but as a vaguely conceived mass. Eros is a potency rather than a person. We are not told how Gaia and Eros came into being. They may symbolize matter and spirit, but they are not derived from Chaos as a higher principle. The ruling principle of the cosmogony is not that of cause and effect, but that of sequence in time. We only hear that Gaia and Eros came afterwards (*epita*). And the same is true of the second pair, Erebus and Night. A step further removed from Chaos are Aether and Day, who are children of Erebus and Night. Thus, in Hesiod's cosmogony we do not find any real attempt to explain the *causes* of things. However, the *purpose* of creation (the provision of a safe home for the gods) and far reaching *abstraction* by which the poet goes back to Space, and then step by step he reconstructs the world, is quite clear.

Pherecydes, a native of Syros, but lived in Athens in the court of Pisistratus (6th century BC), founded an Orphic community at Athens. His own work is lost. However, from its references in the literature we know that he derived the universe from three first principles, Zas (=Zeus), Chronos, and Chthonia (or Chthon). At the summit of the cosmogony, then, stands Zeus. He is regarded as a purely spiritual principle. Chronos, the second member of the trinity, naturally denotes the Time, in which everything happens, and occupies an analogous position to Space in Hesiod's cosmogony. Lastly, Chthonia must be taken to mean either primary matter or the Earth-spirit. All these three principles were alike eternal.

The cosmogony begins when Chronos produces from his seed Fire, Air, and Water, which then in turn beget the five families of the gods. Thus gods and elements alike are the offsprings of Time. And now Zeus-Eros plans to create the world. There is a likeness between the cosmogonies of Pherecydes and Hesiod, but Pherecydes marks an advance. Zeus is a more spiritual conception than Chaos (space), and there is a certain suggestion of science in cosmogony when he names four elements before the formation of the world. Furthermore, Pherecydes treated Eros (love) as a cosmic principle. Zeus-Eros used the elements as materials for his creative work.

Cretan Epimenides (c. 600 BC) for the first time gives us the doctrine of World-Egg in Greek cosmogony, which is so common in the Indo-European cosmology. Since the later Orphic cosmogonies which include (1) Rhapodist Cosmogony, (2) the Cosmogony of Hiernymus and Hellanicus, and (3) Apollonius Rhodus and Alexander of Aphrodisias are quite late in time and of not much importance in understanding the Greek cosmology, I simply skip them. However, I would certainly mention Aristophanes, who in one of his passages depicts the origin of the universe. According to his description, in the beginning were Chaos, Night, Erebus, and Tartarus. Into the bosom of Erebus, Night laid a wind-born egg (*ipinemion pson*) from which, as the seasons rolled, Eros sprang, gleaming with golden wings. Eros blended all things together, and from their union Heaven, Ocean, Earth, and the races of the gods were born. The golden-winged Eros springing from the egg was a part of the oldest Orphic doctrine.

The 'theologians' as Aristotle calls those whose doctrines we have been considering, represent a perfectly distinct phase of Greek thought. Their mind was less scientific than that of the "physiologists". They made a far keener demand for a vivid representation of the origin and development of the world. *Certainly its cosmogony was too vague.*

(b) Philosophical Cosmogonies

The cosmogonies we have examined are quite speculative and hence vague. The Greek philosophers have also tried to explain the world on philosophical principles and in each case from a distinct philosophical point of view. Amongst the earliest Greek philosophers were the natives of Ionia in Asia Minor. Beginning with *Thales,* who flourished at Miletus about 600 BC, each one of the philosophers sought to explain the universe from a single and a material first principle. They could, however, not explain the ultimate cause of the material change because of which the world in all its parts was formed. The reason was that they regarded the cause as inherent in the nature of the matter itself.

Heraclitus of Ephesus (c. 500 BC) gave the doctrine of *Logos,* by which he gave expression to the thought that the world-forming process must be guided by intelligence. He taught that all reality is material, and that the primary element is Fire. Logos viewed on its corporeal side was Fire, and Fire viewed on its spiritual side was the Logos. Thus the first principle postulated by him is both material and rational, and it was on this basis that the Stoic cosmogony was afterwards reared. But before that time the great thinkers of Greece had sought to show that the world was framed by God as at once rational and non-material Being, and Heraclitus at least paved the way for that conception when he endowed its First Cause with the attribute of reason.

The first Greek philosopher who traced the world to a non-material agency was *Empedocles* (c. 450 BC). He did it in his doctrine of the four elements, whose movements were determined by the twofold agency of Love and Discord. But Anaxagoras, who, though born rather earlier than Empedocles, probably had the work of the latter before him when he wrote, took a far more important step in the direction of idealism. According to Aristotle it was Anaxagoras who first pointed out the real cause of the movement by which the world was formed. This cause he called *Nous,* or Reason, to which also he seems to have attributed a mainly, if not exclusively, transcendental existence.

The opposition between matter and spirit pointed by Anaxagoras was the chief problem of *Plato's Dialectic*. If the first cause was purely immaterial, how could He act on matter at all so as to create the world? In this question and the answer to it lies the chief significance of the cosmogony, which Plato has set before us in the *Timaeus.* In forming the world, God gave it a Body and also a Soul. (1) *The body.* On certain portions of primary matter, which was formless and chaotic, God imprinted various mathematical 'forms' and 'numbers'. Thus arose the four elements of which the body of the universe was composed. The idea of the divine mathematician, in which Pythagorean influence is plainly visible, runs through the whole account of creation. (2) *The soul.* Plato describes the elements of which the World-Soul was composed of, but his account is highly metaphysical, The first attribute of it is motion which is manifested in the motion of the planets. According to the *Laws* (x. 896 A), the essential quality of soul is self-movement. Further, the soul is the cause of movement in other things, and by movement (*kynisis*) Plato understood every kind of change. The World-Soul, therefore, is the cause, not only of locomotion, but also of separation and combination, growth, decay, and dissolution. The second attribute is of intelligence. The World-Soul apprehends not only ideas, but sensible realities. Plato speaks of the World-Soul as *created.* Probably he thought of an emanational process. Plato's cosmogonical process may be summed as: "At the beginning of Time, God created the Universe. A spirit or soul went forth from him, and inhabited the body, which he redeemed from chaos by imprinting mathematical forms on primordial matter". Thus, it is clear that the Platonic cosmogony was an attempt to explain the world on dualistic principles. Since God as pure thought could have no contact with matter, Plato was obliged to assume for the work of creation some formative principles separate from God himself. Hence the separate existence of the mathematical forms imprinted on matter, and especially of the World-Soul incorporated within it.

Although Aristotle criticized the theory of 'Ideas', which Plato held to exist apart from matter, yet his own doctrine was fundamentally dualistic, as appears from his view of the Divine life as energy of self-contemplation. But after his time the Greek thought swung round the opposite pole. Abandoning the dualism by which mind and matter, subject and object, were opposed to each other's mutually exclusive realities, it sought to explain the world by means of a single principle. This man sought in his own subjective experience. This subjective trend in philosophy is the hallmark of the Greek national life from the times of Alexander the great onwards. Now, the subjective life itself has two sides, the one which is universal and spiritual, and the other which is individual and material. It was on the latter view of man's nature that the Epicureans based both their ethical and their physical theories. The Stoics, on the other hand, appealed in their ethics to man's rational nature, while in their physics they derived world from a material principle. This was an apparent inconsistency. Both the Epicureans and the Stoics had what may be called a materialistic cosmogony, but that of the Stoics is in several ways the more important.

The *Stoic* first principle was akin to the Fire of Heraclitus, but of a subtler nature, a fiery breath (*pnevma*) or ether (*aithir*). Stoics first principle is both matter and force in one. The Stoic cosmogony was the chief attempt made by the Greeks not merely to derive but to *explain* the origin of the world from a purely material first principle. It was ingenius, and its account of the manner in which force works in the material world contained elements of permanent value. But it went too far in treating force as a genetic first principle. Stoic's first principle was an abstraction, which could explain nothing.

The *Neo-Platonists* taught that the ultimate source of being was neither matter nor spirit, but a real unity transcending both. This was a monistic standpoint. It was the subjective standpoint of the later philosophical systems. They found the key to Divine nature solely in the subjective side of human experience, in the unity given to outward impressions by the thinking subject. They taught also that the material is less real and perfect than the ideal world, that intellectual cognition is the pathway to truth and goodness, and the actual contact with these realities is attained only by means of an 'ecstasy', in which the distinction between subject and object disappears. Although Neo-Platonists claim that their doctrine was the direct outcome of Plato's teaching, yet it seems to be more influenced by Oriental thinking. I cannot go on discussing many of the philosophers of this school, Plotinus (AD 204–269) and others, in detail as it is out of our purview of time and the topic. However, it is sufficient to state here that all attempts by Greek theories to explain the origin of the world fail mainly through the abstractness of its first principle—a Unity of which not even Being can be predicated.

In its mysticism the Neo-Platonic theory of the world reminds us not a little of the Orphic cosmogonies. It resembles them, indeed, both in form and in spirit, as might be inferred from the fact that the notices of the latter given by Damascius are interwoven with Neo-Platonic conceptions.

CHAPTER 5

Concept of Justice, Social Justice and Ethics

Justice cannot be cognitively defined, only interest can. The question of what social justice consists in, then, boils down to two central issues: One, what kind of social life and relations can, ideally, be claimed or considered to be the most appropriate for maintaining and sustaining a particular way of life and, two, what is the extent to which the tenor of social life and relations draws its inspiration from individual orientation and behavior conforming to and consciously reflecting and expressing in actual behavior the essential features of conceptually conceived ideal pattern of life.

Locating the discussion in this perspective, I shall focus on: (a) concept and theories of justice; (b) scope and origin of the concept of social justice; (c) the idea of justice in traditional Indian thinking; (d) the idea of *dharma* and its relevance in the traditional Indian social structure; and (e) distributive justice as viewed from the Indian perspective.

THEORIES OF JUSTICE

Justinian gave a general definition of justice which is still relevant. He notes, "Justice is the constant and perpetual will to render to everyone his due". 'Social justice' is a sub-category of the broader concept, 'justice', and can hardly be understood apart from the latter. It is unquestionably accepted that a sense of justice is a very important attribute of individuals as well as societies. The objects of justice cover a very wide range. Although we frequently make judgments about just people, acts, etc., usually, our judgments are prompted by our perception of injustice in them. Therefore, in order, to get a preliminary idea of what justice might be, it may be useful to think of situations which we typically characterize as 'unjust'. Robbery, criminal act against a person, institutional discrimination in employment on the grounds of color of the skin or sex, unequal distribution of profits amongst the individuals of a cooperative society, or a group of people suffering from hunger while another group is consuming a large quantity, etc. may be instances of injustice. Then what is justice? Justice has a great deal to do with 'fittingness', 'fairness', 'proportion', and so on.

Non-rational sentient beings cannot be said to be capable of discriminating between just and unjust acts, for that matter, of making judgements of any sort, and hence of acting justly or unjustly. Only a special kind of sentient being, the species of humans, can be said to *commit* injustices. Judgements of justice or injustice are moral judgements, whenever they are not merely legal; and since rationality is a pre-condition of morality, only a rational being can be just or unjust.

This connection of justice with morality also implies that the typical context of justice, like that of morality, is social. It has a social context because it is the arena where action takes place for the realization of different purposes by different individuals and groups. This increases the possibility of tension and conflict because of the lack of homogeneity in human purposes. In a world inhabited by a single being, question of justice or injustice would not arise, nor those of morality or immorality. But given the context of a society, an individual may be judged to have, or to lack, principles, dispositions, or habits which make for or militate against a just state of affairs in the society. Hence justice can be said to be the virtue of individuals as well as societies. There may be societies where the question of justice or injustice may not arise at all, for example, a society of saints or, as Hume points out, a society with profuse abundance of the external conveniences, or in a society of friends. Typically, therefore, the context of justice presupposes unfulfilled needs and wants, unequal competition for scarce goods and resources. Rivalry for rewards and privileges, and, very importantly, the urge for power and prestige. In other words, the more imperfect the world, the greater its need for justice.

John Rawls (1964, p.132) also regards 'justice' as a virtue of social institutions, or what he calls 'practice'...as a sort of technical term meaning any form of activity specified by a system of rules which defines offices, roles, moves, penalties, defenses, and so on, and which gives the activity its structure. Individuals or societies may be spoken of as being just or unjust, in recent philosophy, justice is typically regarded as a virtue of social institutions.

Hans Kelsen (1957) regards three types of the theory of justice best known in the modern times (Libertarian, Liberal, and Socialist) as *rationalistic,* as against those that he calls '*metaphysical-religious*'. The distinction between these two very broad classes of theories rests on how each class of theories is justified. Rationalist theories, whatever the differences among them, justify their concept of justice, its priority among other virtues, and its principles by claiming that they are the products of human reason. What rationalistic theories do not do is to postulate or imply any metaphysical or religious entities, properties, virtues, or processes whose existence could be required for the derivation of either the concept or the principle of justice. Metaphysical-religious theories, on the other hand, do make such a postulation. Plato stands out as the kind of thinker for whom the ultimate justification for justice in this world is the fact that, in a world beyond this one, that is, in the world of Forms, there exists a form of justice. Perfect justice, like perfect beauty, is not to be found in this world, and what little there is of it here is so because it is a poor reflection of its 'master-original', the form of justice. This form of justice itself, however, is an integral part of the form of the good, the highest reality in Plato's scheme, comparable in many ways to the theistic idea of God. Religions, in like fashion, provide justification for justice by claiming it to be an attribute of God. It is important to be just because we are God's children and He is just.

According to Hans Kelsen (1957) this division between the rationalistic and the metaphysical-religious applies even to the so-called natural law theories of justice which were proposed during the seventeenth and eighteenth centuries. Natural law theories regard justice to be an integral part of the constitution of nature in general, and of human nature in particular. Nature, thus, becomes a model of the laws of justice and order; by analyzing nature, we can discover the norms prescribing the just conduct of human beings. If nature is regarded as created by God, then the laws of nature are regarded as the expression of the will of God. If, however, natural law is regarded as being deducible from human reason alone, then there is no need to see it as rooted in any transcendental entities or processes. Thus there is no good reason to think that natural theories herald the breakdown of the division between the two broad classes of theories outlined above.

Aristotle may be regarded as the father of the rationalistic type, appealing as it does, not to any transcendental reality but to common sense or human reason in decisions concerning justice. We owe to him the distinction between justice as the whole of virtue and justice as a particular virtue. In the former sense, being just is synonymous with being virtuous or moral. The religious notion of righteousness seems to be closer to this sense of justice. But, as a particular virtue, justice means fairness or equality: one is just in this sense if one does not take more than one's due. Aristotle's thinking about justice in this latter sense is a direct corollary of his more general theory about virtue itself, particularly of his doctrine of the 'golden mean'. Justice, likewise, is the mean between too much and too little. In his own words:

> Just action is intermediate between doing injustice and suffering injustice. Since the former is to get too much and the latter is to get too little. Justice is a sort of middle state, but not in the same manner as the other virtues are middle state; it is middle because it attaches to a middle amount, injustice being the quality of extremes. Also justice is the virtue which disposes the just man to resolve to act justly, and which leads him, when distributing things between himself and another, not to give himself a larger portion and his neighbor a smaller one of what is desirable....In an unjust distribution to get too little is to suffer injustice and to get too much is to do injustice (Aristotle, 1980, p. 21).

It should be clear that Aristotle is here referring, directly at any rate, to what he calls 'distributive' justice, which relates to the distribution of goods, such as money, honors etc., among people according to their desert. Aristotle's thoughts provide the backdrop to some modern discussion trends about issues of social justice. Modern theories of positive justice can be conveniently studied under three broad headings: (a) Liberal, (b) Libertarian, and (c) Socialist. Contractual Liberalism of Kant and John Rawls, Utilitarian Liberalism of Mill and Libertarianism of Nozick, and Socialism of Marx are the representatives of these three schools.

So far as the metaphysical-religious conception of justice is concerned, it is exemplified in all the religions of the world. But here we are concerned only with the Indian tradition. We will discuss the same when dealing with the topic. But, here it will suffice to say that since the primary purpose of religion is the moral and spiritual transformation of human nature, it ought not to be construed as a direct instrument of social justice on earth, as it is by Liberation theologians, for example, and by many liberal Christians and Jews. Indirectly, however, religion may well be a precondition of social justice. For, it can be argued that, in the absence of the counteracting effects of the moral and spiritual values prescribed by religion, the liberal vision of individual rights and social justice may be self-defeating. The conditions for social justice are maximized when two conflicting utopias—liberalism, on the one hand, and metaphysical-religious ideas of justice on the other hand—act as much-needed counterweights to each other.

WHAT IS SOCIAL JUSTICE?

In *Theories of Justice* Brian Barry provides a systematic and detailed analysis of two kinds of answers. One is that justice arises from a sense of the advantage to everyone of having constraints on the pursuit of self-interest. The other answer connects the idea of justice with that of impartiality. The debate about social justice began in 1971 with John Rawls (1958) when he said:

> The principles of justice may...be regarded as those principles which arise when the constraints of having a morality are imposed upon parties in the typical circumstances of justice.

These ideas are, of course, connected with a familiar way of thinking about justice which goes back at least to the Greek Sophists, and which regards the acceptance of the principles of justice as a compromise between persons of roughly equal power who would enforce their will on each other if they could, but who, in view of the equality of forces amongst them and for the sake of their own peace and security, acknowledge certain forms of conduct insofar as prudence seems to require. Justice is thought of as a pact between rational egoists the stability of which is dependent on a balance of power and a similarity of circumstances. (Perhaps the best known statement of this conception is that given by Glaucon at the beginning of Book II of Plato's *Republic*.... In modern times elements of the conception appear in a more sophisticated form in Hobbes *The Leviathan* and in Hume *A Treatise of Human Nature*). While the account (in "Justice and Fairness") is connected with this tradition and with its most recent variant, the theory of games, it differs from it in several important respects....

[T]he acceptance of the duty of fair play by participants in a common practice is a reflection in each person of the recognition of the aspirations and interests of the others to be realized by their joint activity....[The] main purpose [of these remarks] is to forestall...the misinterpretation that on the view presented, the acceptance of justice and the acknowledgement of the duty of fair play depend in everyday solely on there being a *de facto* balance of forces between the parties. It would indeed be foolish to underestimate the importance of such a balance in securing justice; but it is not the only basis thereof. The recognition of one another as a person with similar interests and capacities engaged in a common practice must, failing a special explanation, show itself in the acceptance of the principles of justice and the acknowledgement of the duty of fair play.

Barry has made a critical analysis of the two theories of justice that seem to be leading contenders: one calls justice as mutual advantage and the other justice as impartiality. He argues that people who have not been exposed to the arguments of a Hobbes or a Gauthier will naturally tend to reject out of hand the notion that justice is nothing more than a matter of mutual advantage. It is true that the exact specification of justice as impartiality would not naturally occur to someone who had not given the question much thought. The general idea of justice as impartiality is a systematization of everyday forms of moral argument. The question about the justice of institutions arises when the authority of customs weakens its hold on the minds of the members of a society. As it comes to be perceived that social, political, and economic inequalities are the product of human conventions, the need for justification is felt. Two responses that have been developed deny that social inequality is based on convention. One seeks to find the basis of social inequalities as natural, a line of argument that can be traced from Aristotle's defense of slavery to modern "scientific" racism. The other seeks a metaphysical basis for social inequalities: from the elaboration of the Hindu system to the Church of England's complacent belief that God "ordered" the "estate" of rich and poor, the major religions have a remarkable record of supporting whatever system of inequalities happens to prevail at the time.

Barry thinks that neither of these forms of justification for inequality will do. He goes on to argue that if we set the problem up as one of justifying inequality on the assumption that it is the product of human convention and not underwritten by any deep natural or metaphysical inequality between human beings, there are not a lot of potential solutions. At the highest level of generality, there are perhaps only two. Both start from the idea that conventions that are adhered to are preferable to unrestrained conflict. They then diverge in what they ask of a satisfactory convention. One line says that the convention must be acceptable to each person when he consults his own advantage. The other says that it must be acceptable to everyone when he takes up an impartial standpoint. He traces the first tradition from the Sophists through Hobbes to Gauthier and second from the Stoics through Kant to Rawls. For the first alternative, the key development has been the invention of game theory and its increasingly flexible deployment in social analysis. For the second alternative, it has been the notion, put forward by Rawls, of an original position, conceived of as ethically privileged choice situation. The level of sophistication with which Hobbes is treated has been raised immeasurably in the past three decades, and we are also beginning to see a reevaluation of the social contract tradition in the light of Rawls's work. Both approaches are implicit in the theories of both Hume and Rawls.

Thus, it is clear that social justice is relatively a new concept in political science as well as in social sciences. It has come into wide usage in the latter part of the 20th century even though its roots can be traced back into history. The emergence of this concept in the vocabulary is due, largely, to the fact that the advent and development of liberal democracy failed to solve one of the basic problems of class-ridden society, viz. the problem of narrowing the gap between the haves and the have-nots, the privileged and the deprived. The concept of social justice draws attention to this weakness of liberal democracy and calls for a social order in which everyone is treated with justice and fairness.

Social justice is an application of the concept of distributive justice to the wealth, assets, privileges, and advantages that accumulate within a society or state because the essence of justice is the attainment of the common goods as distinguished from the goods of individuals even of the majority. There have been two major conceptions of social justice, one embodying the notion of merit and desert, the other those of needs and equality. The first conception involves ending of hereditary privileges and an open society in which people have the chance to display their desert. It is expressed in 'equality of opportunity' and 'careers open to talents'. The second conception implies that goods should be allocated according to each person's varied needs. As it aims to make people materially equal, it entails an idea of equality.

The concept of social justice suffers from a certain degree of vagueness. It is capable of meaning different things to different persons. Some ingredients of the concept are, however, easy to identify. Social justice involves the creation of a just and fair social order, just and fair to one and all. To make the social order just and fair for every member of the community, it may be necessary for those who are privileged to make some sacrifices for the sake of the good of unprivileged ones. In this sense, social justice is a revolutionary ideal. However, it does not mean the pulling down of some to make them equal to others. On the contrary, it means the pulling up of those who, for any reason, are weak and underprivileged and who have been left behind in the race of life. While social justice does not envisage the reduction of everyone to a level of flat equality in terms of economic resources and political status, it does imply the balancing of the interests of the individual with those of society. In short, it can be said that social justice helps in bringing about a just society. Social justice includes both economic justice and social justice.

Social justice is not a blind concept or an irrational dogma. It seeks to do justice to all the citizens of the state. As soon as the ideal of a welfare state is accepted by democracy, it leads to one important consequence, and, that is, the claims of social justice must be treated as paramount and primary and if the freedom of the individual and his individual rights need to be regulated in order to achieve social justice, that regulation is a part of the price which democratic citizens must cheerfully pay in order to sustain the democratic way of life. Social justice has a special significance in the context of Indian society as the Hindu society is divided into castes and communities which create walls and barriers of exclusiveness and proceed on the basis of considera-tions of superiority and inferiority. This social inequality presents a serious problem to Indian democracy. The concept of social justice thus takes within its sweep the objective of removing all inequalities and affording equal opportunities to all citizens in social affairs as well as economic activities.

In India, justice is a generic term which includes both procedural and substantive justices: the former providing rules of court of procedure and mechanism what is generally known as *natural justice* and the latter making provision for social assistance, benefits, facilities, concessions, privileges, and special rights to those who deserve and need such help described by the omnibus term *social justice.*

THE IDEA OF JUSTICE IN INDIAN TRADITION

(a) Hinduism

The classical Indian literature is concerned largely with this aspect of the idea of justice and relates this idea directly to another seminal idea, that of *dharma.* The idea of *dharma* is the later day version of *Rita*, the Vedic conception of cosmic order which, when imitated in individual and social beings, maintains both social order and individual fulfillment. When translated in social terms, *dharma* connotes both *sadharana* and *varnashrama dharma.*

It is the expression of these two facets of *dharma* in individual lives and social relations that is claimed, in the traditional Indian thinking, as conducive to justice.

Hindu conception of justice—whether in the sense of individual righteousness, or a moral and social order which is our duty to preserve—seems to spring, directly or indirectly, from the *Rig Vedic* notion *rta,* which denotes primarily the cosmic order, and, by implication, the order of the moral law, on the one hand, and the 'causal' order of the performance of sacrifices, on the other. Its centrality and importance in the *Rig Veda,* is clear and abundant. The gods themselves are born of the *rta*, and they follow the *rta*; they are practisers of *rta* and knowers of it. *Varuna*, the chief god of the Hindu pantheon is its special guardian and truth its special expression. To be a follower of *rta* is to inculcate certain virtues: 'consideration in domestic relations, political loyalty, truth in friendship, abstention from crimes such as theft and murder and fidelity in marriage, especially demanded of women'. In the *Brahmanas,* the ritualistic portions of the Vedas, these moral virtues are interspersed with sacerdotal virtues—the importance of maintaining the purity of sacrifices and avoiding 'sins' that follow from their improper performance. Early Vedic society had a highly developed moral consciousness which was integrally bound up with religious consciousness. Man must act as the Gods act and the Gods act by a fixed and eternal law called *rta*. Thus the ideas of Natural Law, at once moral and cosmic, was developed early. *Rta* and *satya*, law and truth, were thus held to be the foremost virtues. The belief in *rta* produced a belief in a just ritual order for all human life and actions. Social life was thus sought to be regulated ritually and sacramentally (G.C. Pande, 1984, pp. 126–127). This reutilization of social ethics remained a permanent part of the tradition of *dharma* later on. Not only does the notion of *rta* lead to a ritualized scheme of social ethics, it makes piety the first of all virtues. Piety implies faith or *sraddha*, 'placing the heart' or placing in the heart. It implies further attuning the mind (*dhi*) to the will of the gods and the readiness to serve them. Truth or *satya* is often mentioned as coordinated with *rta*. They were the first-born of the creative effort of the gods. "By Truth is the earth upheld, the heaven propped up"

(*R.V.X.85,41*). Truth meant the conformity of thoughts to the natural law and the conformity of speech and action to the mind. Truth is opposed to lying or deceit or crookedness (Pande, 1984, p. 128).

In the *Smritis* and *Upanishads,* the historically later sections of sacred literature, this concept gives way to the cognate concept of *dharma* which stands for the cosmic order, the law, justice, morality, and the very fabric of social order. One who follows *dharma* acquires merit of promoting the natural order. Although ritual and sacerdotal duties are still commanded as being one's *dharma*, moral and social virtues are emphasized too, especially in the *Grhya* and *Dharma sutras*: truth, abstention from injury to the persons or properties of others, charity, hospitality, courage and devotion to duty, and so on, being the main virtues. Those failing to obey the dictates of *dharma* are threatened with punishment in the future life and the virtuous and just are promised rewards in like manner. The doctrine of *Karma*, that is, that a man's place in life is determined by his deeds in a former life and his moral or immoral actions in this *life* will determine his status and character in future lives, is seen as a corollary of the 'Natural Law', or *dharma*. Upholding *dharma* in all its manifestations—including, very importantly, the duties and obligations emanating from one's 'natural' place in society, that is, one's *varna* and *asrama* (stage in life)—is upholding justice and social order. Transgressions are threatened with punishment not only in the form of a 'low' birth in another life, but also of a possible descent into hell, the kingdom of *Yama*. While upholding *dharma*, or the moral order, it is extremely important, there is no doubt, however, that one's supreme end, *summum bonum,* is not *dharma*, but *moksha,* or liberation from the worldly cycle (*Sansara*), to be gained chiefly through 'knowledge' but also through devotion and 'action'. The practice of *dharma* itself can be a stepping stone to *moksha*, the highest goal. In the *Upanishads* appears also the doctrine that all individual souls (*atman*) are parts of one universal soul (*Brahman*), with which or into which they merge on liberation. Manu (XII.125) has clearly stated this: "He who thus recognizes the Self through the Self in all created beings, becomes equal (-minded) towards all, and enters the highest state, Brahman" (F. Max Muller (ed.): *Sacred Books of the East*, Vol. XXV, The Laws of Manu, p. 513). This idea of *atman* and *Brahman* provides at the same time the rationale, on the one hand, for the equal treatment of others—the cornerstone of justice—and on the other, for the downgrading of earthly morality and justice, denying distinctions of any sort of liberated stage.

Pande (1984, p. 126, n. 2) says that the 'notion *dharma* embodies the tradition of the pursuit of moral values and constitutes one of the most distinct and essential aspects of Indian culture. The concept of *dharma* is not merely theoretical but intensely practical. Embodied in rules and institutions and illustrated by popular character-types from epic stories, Puranic myths and legends and folk-tales, the notion of *dharma* reaches every man, the illiterate peasant and housewife as much as the learned philosopher and minister. *Dharma* like *sadhana* is one of those golden threads which bind the elite and the common folk together and which are available at the level of everyday life but reach up to heavens'. Pande further argues that Hegel's *Sittlichkeit* or 'social ethics' is very near to the concept of *dharma* which includes morality and law, convention and courtesy. "Revelation, tradition and convention have all gone into the making of *dharma* which thus constitutes the essential social bond". It is called *dharma* because it is the principle of cohesion (*dharma*). "*Dharma* holds the people together" (*Dharanad dharma ityahuh Dharma dharhyate prajah*). Pande is of the opinion that 'it is a precise reversal of the current behaviorist and positivist outlook of the social sciences. What determines social form is the apprehension of 'Ideal law'. The *Purusha-sukta* traces the social order to the divine *purusha*. While Brahmanical tradition continued to advocate the importance of the sacerdotal, ritual, and esoteric aspects of *dharma*, the morality of popular Hindu culture found its expression in the epic literature, especially in the two great epics, the *Ramayana* and the *Mahabharata*. Not only precepts of personal righteousness but also the ideals of social and political action for the preservation of justice issued from these great books, as exemplified by the heroes of these popular stories. The most celebrated of these sources is *Gita*, which, although only a part of the *Mahabharata* (and so not 'revealed' literature) still ranks among Hindus as a source of great authority and respect, especially on the question of justice and duty. Not only does it provide the philosophical ground for altruistic and compassionate action by emphasizing the unity of all beings in *Isvara* (God), of whom Krishna is an incarnation, it also offers a deontological justification of social action, in a dramatic setting. Arjuna must fight his *Kaurava* cousins inspite of the killing of kith and kin involved, because as a *Kshatriya* prince, it his duty to fight for justice, whatever the consequences. Duty is to be done simply because it is duty and not because certain consequences might or might not follow from it. Personal inclination has no place in the context of the duty to restore justice (*dharma*). This exhortation to do battle because it is right to do so also enunciates, indirectly, the doctrine of a 'just war'. As if these personal exhortations were not enough, Krishna reinforces it with his exposition of the purpose of divine incarnation: God (personified here by Krishna himself) incarnates himself from age to age for the protection of the good, the destruction of the evil, and the establishment of *dharma*, or justice. That this *dharma* consists primarily in performing, in a non-attached way, the duties of one's own *Varna* and *asrama*, is not in doubt. But the fact is that *dharma* which represents personal duty is also at the same time the 'natural' order, the moral law, the repository of justice and virtue.

The theory of four *Varnas* finds its *locus classicus* in the *Purusha-sukta* (*R.V: X.*90). Here *Purusha* is the source of cosmos as of society. 'There is a correspondence between the functional parts of *Purusha* and the *varnas* in society. The order of the *varnas* thus comes to be an organic unity and the relationship of the different *varnas* too forms a hierarchy. Spiritual authority, temporal power, production of wealth, and labor are the four chief social functions where the first two were pre-eminent while the last two were held as necessities rather than values' (Pande, 1984, p. 134). Although society consists of four orders, it is held together and flourishes by the principle of *dharma*. *Dharma* is the same as truth, and speaking truth is speaking justly. Both these, "Truth and Justice, are the same". (*Brihadaranyaka*, 4.4.14).

According to the *Dharmasastra*, *dharma* as virtue consists in everyone doing one's duty according to one's own station. Correspondingly, social justice consists in keeping the orders (*varnas*) distinct and unmixed. The prevention of social miscegenation or confusion (*samkara*) was thus regarded as the principal value to be realized in the maintenance of public life. In essentials, this idea of non-confusion is comparable to the 'platonic idea of justice and the Confucian idea of the Rectification of Names' (Pande, 1984, p. 160). Unfortunately, the identification of functional classes with rigid hereditary groups produced a system of 'castes' which could neither be fully real nor represent the ideal. This was a plain perversion of the notion of *dharma* and was criticized by liberal and enlightened thinkers. The *Mahabharata* and Buddhist and Jain works reflect this critical and enlightened outlook which protested against the perversion of the notion of 'social order' (Pande, 1984, p. 161).

Thus conceived, says Pande, 'society was held to be engendered by a primordial sacrifice which was regulated by the first Laws or *Dharmas*'. The *Varnas* were created for the sake of work. That work called *Dharma* regulates everyone's duty and is the means of obtaining human ends and values" (Sankara, *Isadi-dasopanisadah*, p. 694 (ad. *Br*.4.15)). *Dharma* came to replace the early Vedic concept of *Rta*. If *Brahman* is the original substance of creation in its ultimate unity, *dharma* is the law that governs the created world in its dynamic inter-relationship. It is the law that underlies nature as well as society. *Dharma* is the ruler of the ruler. Therefore, there is nothing higher than *dharma*. (Pande, 135). *Sreyas* or the moral good is identified with *dharma* which is explained as the principle of social justice grounded in truth. The word *Dharma* corresponded to the Greek conception of justice or *dike* and there is an obvious similarity between the platonic explanation of justice and the conception of *dharma* as the just social order correlating human classes based on aptitude and functions (for a detailed analysis of platonic conception, see Roy (2000, pp. 1–5). Even the hierarchy of the classes is the same except that the Indian conception distinguishes the philosopher from the king and would keep them distinct. *Dharma* came to be defined as a system of rules deriving their authority from the Vedic tradition and regulating personal conduct as well as social relations and business. Manu uses the word *dharma* beyond *Varnasramadharma* to include also the rules and customs current in different regions, castes, and families also.

Desa-dharman Jatidharman kuladharmansca sasvatan Pasanda-gana-dharmansca sastre sinnuktavanmanuh (Manu, 1.118). *Varnasrama dharma* itself includes *Varnadharma, asram dharma, Varnasrama-dharma, gunadharma and naimittika dharma* (Manu, 2.25, *cf. Bhavisyapurana)*.

Manusmriti completed the task which *Sutras* had begun and it did it so well that in practice it replaced them. Unlike the *Sutras*, the *Maunsmriti* is not only detailed and systematic but places the rules of *dharma* within a theoretical structure.

Anoher idea of particular significance in the context of justice that occurs to be in the epic group of literature is the notion of 'the golden age', the age of justice, peace, and plenty. Any particular world, according to Hinduism, passes through various ages, epochs, or phases. Manu begins with the account of creation which depends on the *Nasadiya* and *Purusha-suktas.* The account is Vedantic but takes the help of Samkhya too. Creation is bound by the dualities of pleasure and pain. Underlying these is the distinction of right and wrong actions. There is succession of four human ages *Krta, Treta, Dvapara,* and *Kali*. These take up a total of twelve thousand years, a modest figure which the commentators and later understanding inflate fantastically by interpreting the years to be 'divine years' (Pande, 1984 p. 140). *Krtayuga* was a golden age when the *dharma* was in full swing. In each succeeding age, a quarter of *dharma* was lost. *Tapas* was the principle *dharma* in *Krta* age, *jnana* in the *Treta, yajna* in *Dvapara,* and *dana* in Kali. It starts with *Krta,* the golden age, or the age of truth *(Satya Yuga)*, but then, like any other constructs, begins to decay and abound in evil and injustice, until at last, in the 'degenerate Yuga' *(Kali Yuga)*, it is only fit for destruction, to be followed by the 'recreation' of another world. The significance of this golden age idea is that it provides a source of ideals of justice, personal righteousness as well as social justice, not unlike the biblical idea of the Kingdom of God.

It was certainly a focal point in Mahatma Gandhi's formulation of just social order: his adoption of the term *Rama Rajya,* or the kingdom of Rama, while providing him with inspiration in spelling out his vision of a just social and political order, allowed him, at the same time, to harness popular support for his cause through the use of a popular but ancient concept. Gandhi, as well as some of the other modern social reformers of India, undoubtedly influenced by the active social ethics of Christianity, delved into the epics to fish out ideas and concepts that would allow them to counteract the distinctly other-worldly philosophy of renunciation that had become dominant in the Hinduism of India at the time. To Gandhi, at least, while the *Ramayana* provided the idea of *Rama Rajya*, the Kingdom of God, the *Gita* furnished the basis of positive political action in the establishment of a just order and the removal of imperialism and injustice, as it did also for Tilak and certain other freedom fighters and reformers.

(b) Buddhism

Buddhism, at least early Buddhism, views righteousness as well as the idea of a just social order within the framework of the three Hindu concepts of *dharma, karma, and nirvana.* As a non-theistic religion, it views righteousness as conformity, not with divine dictates, but with 'laws' of the natural order *(dharma)*. Good actions which earn merit, therefore, are actions which are in keeping with this order: 'In the organic universe, right and wrong, and those consequences of actions which we call justice, retribution, compensation, are as truly and inevitably a part of the eternal natural or cosmic order as the flow of a river, the process of the seasons' (Rhys Davids, C.A.F.: *Buddhism*, p. 118). The 'law' of *karma* is unyielding, so that right action always leads to a reward and wrong action to punishment. According to the Hinayana school, the ideal aim of its followers is the life of a saint *(arhat)*: 'one who has become independent of the universe and free from any desire for it'. But in the Mahayana schools, while the ideal of the *arhat* is never explicitly abandoned, it seems to be gradually transcended by a superior ideal, that is, of becoming a *bodhisattva.* Everyone is potentially a Buddha, and by right resolve and action, but especially by the thought of enlightenment, one may, through numberless existences, eventually become Buddha. A *bodhisattva* is one who, '.... has for numberless aeons practiced the good conduct of well-done *karma*, aims, morality, patience, fortitude, meditation, wisdom, resource, learning, conduct, vows and penance; he is endowed with great friendliness, compassion and sympathy; in his mind has arisen equanimity, and he strives for the weal and happiness of all the beings' (*Vajracchedika Sutra)*. The most fruitful idea to emerge from the concept of the *bodhisattva*—at least in the context of altruism and the creation of a just social order—is that of his compassion (*Karuna)* for all beings: he will not forsake his fellow creatures. The *bodhisattvas* have compassion, because, in their wisdom they perceive the interconnectedness of things and beings, and the futility of the idea of individual liberation. The transformation of *Buddha* into the *bodhisattva,* and the declaration of a community of beings, all sharing a common destiny and operating under a common causal nexus, the law of *karma,* is the main theme of the Mahayana Buddhism. The *Bodhisattva* is greatly moved by the spectacle of the misery of the people around him—the worldlings deluded by ignorance. They are attached to sensual pleasures and are enslaved by egotism, pride, false opinion, lust etc., and know no rest. The plight of the worldlings moves the Bodhisattva to pity and compassion. Determined to help the creatures, he reflects:

> Whatever Good I have acquired by doing all this, may I (by the merit) appease and assuage all the pains and sorrows of all living beings. . . . May I be like unto a healing drug for the sick. . . . May I allay the pain of hunger and thirst by showers of food and drink . . . renounce my bodies, my pleasure and my Merit in the past, present and future, so that all beings may attain the Good . . . May I be the protector of the helpless. May I be the guide of wayfarers. May I be a boat, a bridge and a cause bay for all who wish to cross (stream). May I be a lamp for all who need a lamp. May I be a bed for all who lack a bed. May I be a slave to all who want a slave (Hardayal: 1970, pp. 57–58).

Both *Advaita* Vedanta and the Mahayana School of Buddhism believe in the possibility of *Jivanmukti* (liberation in lifetime) for the person who has attained right vision or the true insight into the nature of things.

The emphasis on *ahimsa* as the main constituent of righteousness or *dharma* is another important element in the Buddhist humanism. It is considered not merely as a negative measure preventing injury to creatures but also as contributing positively to their well-being (*yad ishad api paropakarkam tat sarvam apy ahimsantas samvihitam*).

Commenting on a verse in *Chatuhsataka* of Aryadeva (XII.23) *Chandrakirti* observes: "That which is helpful to others in any measure, is all included within Ahimsa".

In the *Assalayana Sutta,* Buddha is represented as upholding emancipation for all the *varnas* (*caturvanim Siddhim)* as the system is itself not natural. The societies have only two classes—freemen and slaves. In the moral realm, laws are applied equally to all the *varnas* and their destiny is determined by the quality of their deeds, not by the accident of their birth in life. All men constitute the same species. In the *Vasettha sutta* Buddha points out the difference between species and caste and concludes that the distinction among human beings rests on vocation. One does not become a Brahman or a non-Brahman by birth. It is by deeds that one becomes or ceases to be a Brahmana. In the *Sundarka-bharadvaja sutta Buddha* says, "do not ask about birth, ask about conduct" [*ma jatim pucchi caranam ca puccha, (Khuddaka* I, pp. 334)]. The Buddhist held that human nature is naturally good and that the source of evil is the force of untamed desire. What makes a person valuable is the degree of his enlightenment, not social position. In the *Vajrasuci* attributed to Ashvaghosha it is said that "Brahmanhood is not by scriptures, or sacraments or *birth* or family or Vedic learning or profession. Brahmanhood is the avoidance of sins". In fact, all men belong to the same race. There is only one human order or world which gets functionally divided into four. The Jainas too have similar tradition with respect to the question of social distinction depending on social functions. There is only one human *jati* which becomes many *varnas* through functional differences (*vrittibheda)* (Pande, 65–66).Thus, it can be safely concluded that the teachings of both Buddhism and Jainism have a direct bearing on any consideration of social justice.

This in short is a survey of the more important contributions of the Indian tradition toward a humanistic outlook on life, basically important for any consideration of social justice, to be met within the rich Indian tradition of religio-philosophic thought—ancient and modern. The importance attached to the category of *Atman* in the Upanishads and the systems of metaphysical thought deriving from them, to existential suffering in Buddhism and to the ideal of *Jivanmukti* in the entire range of spiritual reflections provide solid basis for the development of the philosophy of social justice.

RELIGION AND SOCIAL JUSTICE

Religion is man's response to the totality of meanings involved in the possibilities of his finite existence; it is a device to adjust to that totality in a manner that would make life bearable and possibly cheerful. There are two broad categories of religions, the religion of faith (and worship) and the religion of knowledge and wisdom. As faith that is directed on a deity it may tend to dissociate man from the affairs of the world and the service of man: a sense of detachment is also characteristic of the man of wisdom. But the man of faith may serve humanity if he believes that by doing so he would please his God; and the wise man, driven by his sense of compassion, may actively set about to enlighten humanity.

The two sorts of religious career are exemplified in a superlative degree in the lives of Gautam Buddha and Mahatma Gandhi. Substitute the impulse for higher and nobler life, or truth, as Gandhi calls it, for traditional godhead, and you have the humanistic religion with accent on both service of humanity and the acquisition of knowledge and wisdom. Whether a person believes in God or not, philosophic wisdom involves a measure of detachment toward purely personal concerns. Among world religions Buddhism lays greatest and most systematic emphasis on the metaphysical doctrine of egolessness and cultivation of non-egotism.

Some degree of detachment toward the personal, consciously cultivated and nourished, enables a person to be impartial and just. A measure of religion or religiousness is a prerequisite of effective cultivation of the higher cultural self, consisting in realized vision of truth and beauty. To be religious in our sense is to be lifted up and above the level of merely biophysical existence, into a region where cultivated human person enjoys a common spiritual being or existence.

It is man's capacity for detachment that prompts and enables him to build institutions providing for justice and the conditions of harmonious living. This attitude if extended to the community and ultimately to nations, the cultivation of the virtue of detachment by world leaders in economic and political fields is likely to contribute to the establishment, through the enforcement of truly just and equitable norms of conduct, harmonious relations among classes and nations.

I am of the opinion that even in the context of social justice in its narrow, specialized sense, religion may have an indirect, but beneficial, role to play, insofar as it succeeds in instilling moral values in humans and in weaning them away from mere material concerns, thus curbing their tendency toward heedless consumerism, selfishness, and greed. Personal righteousness is very much the concern of religion: and it can be argued that a society in which righteousness prevails, would tend to have less injustice, even of the economic and political kind. According to no less a figure than Adam Smith:

> (Men) could safely be trusted to pursue their own self-interest without undue harm to the community not only because of restrictions imposed by law, but also because they were subject to built-in restraint derived from morals, religion, custom and education (Quoted in Hirsch, 1977, p. 137).

J.S. Mill (1969, Vol. X, p. 415) also says that 'as a supplement to human laws, (religion) is a more cunning sort of police. Sociologists too accept the importance of religion and the attendant morality in holding society together and keeping it caring. As Hirsch says, ' The functional aspect of religion has always been prominent in the sociological approach; Comte stressing the contribution of belief and ritual in social solidarity and Durkheim the role of religion in inducing participation in social life'. But it is not just because of the intimate connection between morality and religion that the latter becomes important. There may be additional, and perhaps even more, important reasons. As Peter Berger says, . . . 'Man does *not* live by bread alone. He also needs the life-giving and meaning-giving sustenance that no 'naturalist' view of the world can provide. If you will, man needs religion, and if that is so, no technocratic design for human life can be finally satisfactory". Individuals with a sense of transcendence may, on the whole, be much better equipped to create a just society than a bunch of them unable to see beyond their immediate economic goals.

Apart from serving as a source of morality in general, religion may have a special role—an indirect, but perhaps indispensable one, again—if economic development is to lead to social justice. For, as Hirsch points out, the pursuit of individual self-interest, the basis of capitalist enterprise, does not by itself lead to the social good: 'Rather than pursuit of self-interest contributing to the social good, pursuit of the social good contributes to the satisfaction of self-interest. The difficulty is that the latter pursuit needs to be deliberately organized under existing standards and instincts of personal behavior', a task not easily accomplished without restoring religion to its traditional, pivotal, place in society. It is religion, then, that must help reestablish the primacy of altruistic behavior and the spirit of community, as also of goals higher than material wealth and physical well-being.

Every religion has encouraged the doing of 'good works', such as building hospitals, orphanages, and the homes for the homeless refugees, etc. Traditionally, these works have been inspired by a sense of fellow feeling, compassion, charity, and so on, and not by the need to build just economic and political institutions. These works have played an immensely important role in mitigating the pain and suffering of those who have been dealt with harshly by an uncaring nature or by unjust social and political regimes. These good works, then—'the fruits of the spirit', one might call them—are not, by any means, the least important contributions of religion toward the creation of a just and humane social order.

The Indian tradition of social ethics or *dharma* identifies morality with the cultivation of higher emotions and the performance of socially imposed obligations. In one sense it identifies virtue with knowledge, in another, with the disciplined application of the will. It places much emphasis on ascetic conduct and highlights the struggle between duty and temptation. It encourages much preoccupation with the self so that one could be selfless. At the same time it disparages casuistry and moral doubt and promotes a sense of duty and devotion to rule which tends to be literal and encourages a legalistic attitude.

DISTRIBUTIVE JUSTICE—INDIAN TRENDS

In Hindu sociology the emphasis was on overall welfare of the society. Progress is evolutionary in character and evolution implies ascending on a higher plane. Ascending is possible only when there are no impediments. Social progress thus implies the progress of the whole society. Swami Vivekananda (1947, pp. 6–7) describes this aspect in a masterly manner:

> The solution is not by bringing down the higher but by raising the lower up to the level of the higher. And that, is the line of work that is found in all our books in spite of what you may hear from some people whose knowledge of their own scriptures and whose capacity to understand the mighty plans of the ancients are zero.

The underlying principle of the social life of Manu is the ultimate welfare of the individual and the society which can be attained gradually through the various stages of life and discipline; the idea of social justice in *Manusmriti* is realized through the *Varna* and *Asrama* techniques. The complete social philosophy of Hindus is expressed in these two words *Varna* and *Asrama.* The whole of Hindu law is based on the *Varnasramadharma.* In upholding or maintaining the *Varnasrama* system lies the idea of social justice, i.e., all persons should be made to work according to their capacities but all must be given equal share in the enjoyment of social production. One purpose of *dharma* (law) was to inflict punishment upon those who transgress the *Varnasramadharma.* "Of the members of all the (four) several castes in their order of enumeration, true to the duties of their respective orders, the king has been created the protector".

Sve sve dharme nivistanam sarvesamanupurvasah/
Varnanamasramanam ca raja srstoabhiraksita//
(*Manu.* VII, 35)

Varnasrama plan had for its ideal the social welfare of the entire society which is the distinct feature of Indian culture. The emergence of social welfare concept in ancient India lies in the fact that according to *Dharmasastra* writers, society was the organizational unit in which each member of it occupied a very important place. A *Brahmaṅa* is one who has attained perfect intellectuality and spirituality. The concept of social welfare according to Manu and Indian thought includes the overall welfare of the society. It is so comprehensive a term that the welfare does not stop after providing mere guarantee for food and shelter but it aims at securing for each person the status of a *Brahmana*. The idea of social welfare is contained in different *Sutra* texts which contain the earlier elaborate rules governing the society in regard to religion, domestic duties, and mutual relations between different members of the society. Hence we have the *Srauta Sutra*, the *Grihya Sutra*, and *Dharma Sutra*. All were conceived on the basis of *Varna* and *Asrama*. As the ancient Indian legal philosophy was fully concerned with the society the king was not allowed to ignore the prevailing social conditions of society. As a matter of fact he was equally subject to the rules of law along with the subjects with the difference that certain additional duties, responsibilities, and obligations were imposed on him.

In the Indian view of life the emphasis has always been more on duties rather than on rights. Everyone was to do something for the society, which includes all: humans, beasts, birds, and plants. Under the five duties of a householder (*panchamahayajna* viz. *brahmayajna, pitriyajna, daiva, bhuta, and "Adhyapanam brahmayjnah pitriyajnastu tarpanam/ Homo daivo balir bhauto nryajno, tithipujanam"*, Manu, 3.70) arose a very wide and genuine conception of charity. One should not eat alone but also offer food to the gods, guests, dependents, and ancestors. Man has a moral relationship not only with gods and sages and the departed ancestors but owes hospitality to all men and must assist life in all its forms. Elaborate conventions are prescribed for hospitality. Maidens, young brides, pregnant women, and the sick must receive priority in the matter of feeding. To cook only for oneself is sinful (Manu, 3.115,118). Every action was performed with a view to add to the welfare of the society which to very large extent helped the economic adjustments and re-distribution. It was thus no wonder that in India the society grew out, more of sacrifice than of self-indulgence in luxury. Under the conception of various *vratas* it was the duty of the king to work for the welfare of the people—whatever the cost—*Raja Prakritiranjanat.* It was an Indian king *Ramchandra* who abandoned his wife *Sita* for the sake of his people.

In modern India the precursors of movement for distributive justice in its true sense were Swami Vivekananda (1863–1902), Gandhiji (1869–1948) and others all of whom denounced the discriminatory age-old practice of untouchability, championed the doctrines of material and spiritual equality, renunciation and service to society. It is Swami Vivekananda who made a revolutionary statement when he remarked, 'It is mockery to offer religion to a starving man....a country where millions of people live on flowers of the *mohua* plant and a million or so of Brahmins suck the blood out of these poor people ...' (*Complete Works of Swami Vivekananda*, Vol. 5, p. 45). Swamiji diagnosed *four* principal evils—priest craft, poverty, tyranny, and ignorance from which millions of Indian people were to be saved. Similarly, Gandhiji took the cause of common masses particularly, the untouchables and other weaker sections of society including rural and industrial labor. He proclaimed Swaraj could not be complete unless the lowest and humblest sections got 'all the ordinary amenities of life that a rich man enjoys'. It was the imperative duty of the Government, according to Gandhiji, to ensure adequate livelihood to all Indians. As regards social equality Gandhiji considered untouchability as the greatest blot on Hinduism. He declared, 'If untouchability as a part of Hindu creed I should decline to call myself a Hindu and most decidedly embrace some other faith if it satisfied my highest aspirations' (*Young India*, p. 136).

It is such aura of our social, political, and moral heritage that finally shaped the quality and content of justice which finds a pre-eminent place in our National Charter, the Constitution of India. It is these aforesaid values and ideals which inspired the helmsmen of our National Movement particularly Jawaharlal Nehru and Dr. B.R. Ambedkar. Jawaharlal Nehru drove home that the first task of free India is 'to feed the starving people and clothe the naked masses and to give every Indian fullest opportunity to develop himself, according to his capacity' (Nehru, 1972 Vol. III). Dr. B.R. Ambedkar also pin-pointed the three imperatives to make Indian democracy and Constitution a success. The first thing is to hold fast to constitutional methods for achieving our social and economic objective....It means we must abandon the method of civil disobedience, non-*cooperation* and *Satyagraha*...The second thing we must do is to observe the caution which John Stuart Mill has given to all who are interested in the maintenance of democracy, namely, not to lay their liberties at the feet of even a great man, or to trust him the powers which enable him to subvert their institution...The third thing we must do is not to be content with mere political democracy. We must make our political democracy, a social democracy as well. What does social democracy mean? It means a way of life. These principles of liberty, equality, and fraternity are not to be treated as separate items in a trinity. They form a union of trinity in the sense that to divorce one from the other is to defeat the very purpose of democracy.

Equality of opportunity to all citizens to develop their individual personalities and to participate in the pleasures and happiness of life is the goal of economic justice. Social justice as distinguished from economic justice has a special significance in the context of Indian society. As we are all aware, the Hindu social structure is based on castes and communities which create walls and barriers of exclusiveness and proceed on the basis of considerations of superiority and inferiority. This presents a serious problem to democracy in India. The problem of social justice is as urgent and important in India as is the problem of economic justice. The term social justice in a comprehensive sense includes both economic justice and social justice. The concept of social justice thus takes within its sweep the objective of removing all inequalities and affording equal opportunities to all citizens in social affairs as well as economic activities. To meet the challenges of the Marxism by a democratic way of life by adopting the ideal of a welfare state we have committed ourselves to unceasing pursuit of the doctrine of social justice. Social justice is not a blind concept or an irrational dogma. It seeks to do justice to all the citizens of the state. It is a problem of rationally and harmoniously adjusting to the rival claims of individual liberty and freedom. The Indian thinkers have solved the age-old problem in the past by adopting a doctrine of *Samanvyaya* (harmonious synthesis). Social justice must be achieved by adopting necessary reasonable measures with courage, wisdom, foresight, sense of balance, and fair play to all the interests concerned.

Indian society has ever presented a unique spectacle of the harmony and co-existence of diverse social, ethnic, and religious groups. Each group was thus allowed to preserve its traditional way of life which was also called *dharma*. The multiplicity and separateness of *jatis* was the other side of the coin. While *dharma* as virtue proceeded from the spontaneous knowledge of the heart and led to disciplined and altruistic social behavior, it also stood for the duty laid upon a man by his social position and relationships. Unfortunately, in the later Vedic period and more so in the post-Vedic period, they tended to prevent the original ideal of *Varna* by turning it into *jati*. The functional superiority of Brahamanas was sought to be converted into that of hereditary priesthood. 'As a matter of fact, the notion of *varna* was originally a solvent of the diversity of primitive distinctions of clans and tribes. The re-emergence of *jatis* was a retrograde phenomenon' (Pande, 1984, p. 168). Whereas the rise of the *varna*-system in the Vedic age created a universal society out of primeval particularism, the recognition and expansion of the *jati*-system reintroduced social fragmentation, which met with much resistance from non-Brahmanical and heterodox ideas.

Affection and hospitality, tolerance and acceptance, charity and philanthropy, non-violence and compassion are widely accepted values in the Indian tradition. Virtual autonomy of groups in regulating their accustomed mode of social life and harmony between them have been a marked feature of that tradition. The modern notion of the struggle of the individual against the group or groups against groups, whether classes, races, religions or nations, were largely strangers in the context of the ancient ethos. The freedom which the individual sought was ideal freedom, not the freedom to maximize his competitive gains by any means. Instead of the notion of right, that of duty was pre-eminent. It was accepted that justice means non-discrimination but this did not lead to any notion of social or economic equality. Inequalities in these respects were accepted as inevitable on account of the diversity of human capacities, effects, and virtue (Pande, 1984, pp. 169–170).

From the above discussion it would be clear that the traditional Indian notion of justice is a holistic notion and would not admit splitting into social and trans-social domains. Justice was perceived as something belonging to a higher order than the social. If it is brought down to the social plane, and encased within it and is viewed only in the context of *Varna-Jati* system there would be no scope for the notion of social justice within it. However, as hinted above, the original Vedic social organization allowed sufficient space for the free play of both *guna* and *karma*. These got stifled when conjoining social divisions with birth perverted the system. These perversions were continually criticized since the time of Gautam Buddha by even Hindu commentators of the *Smritis*. During the modern period Rammohan Roy, Vivekananda, Mahatma Gandhi, and a host of others have demanded change in the social structure, and they did it not with the intention of deriving any immediate political advantage. Moreover, justice needs a stronger base than rational adjustment of interests. It is impossible to base justice on any other foundation than a supra-mundane notion of ethics and morality.

THE CONCEPT OF ETHICS

Ethics is the branch of philosophy that is concerned with what is morally good or bad, right and wrong, a synonym for it is moral philosophy. Traditionally, ethics has undertaken to analyze, evaluate, and develop normative moral criteria for dealing with moral problems. In recent years, however, pervasive current in Anglo-American ethics has come under the influence of a new conception of the proper methods and capacities of philosophy in general, viz., that its task is the analysis of language; and on this basis it has come to hold that the concern of the moral philosophers should be restricted to the analytic task, or to "meta-ethics". This task consists in the logical analysis of the meanings of moral concepts and of the methods of supporting moral judgments and thus stands in contrast to the more traditional view, which combined such analytic studies with normative ethics, the view that authentic standards exist. The relation between these two conceptions is an example of the controversies that have always divided moral philosophers on a large variety of basic issues arising not only from within their subjectmatter but also from opposed views about their very study of it.

NATURE, TYPES, AND RELATIONS OF ETHICS

The word ethics signifies not only a certain branch of philosophic study but also the object or subject matter of that study. "Ethics" and "ethical" are often used synonymously with "morals" (or "morally") and "moral", when reference is made indifferently to the ethics or to the morality of a person or a group, to their moral or ethical virtues or qualities. The synonym has a clear etymological basis for the Greek word *ethos,* from which "ethics" is derived, and the Latin word *mores,* from which "morals" is derived, both mean habits and customs. The ethics or morality of persons or groups, however, consists not merely in what they habitually or customarily do but in what they think it is fitting, right, or obligatory to do. Men's actions are often, but not always, a sign of what they believe; their actions may diverge from their beliefs, and both actions and beliefs may differ from what men say they ought to do or believe. Morality contains an ineluctable normative element. Whereas a person may engage in habitual and customary conduct without any effective thought, ethics always involves reflective evaluation or prescription concerning the conduct in question. Even when "customary morality" is spoken of, the reference of the term is not merely to the customs as such—in the sense of regular, repeated sequence of behavior—but also to the view, at least implicitly held by the participants, that what they regularly do is in some way right; it is not merely what is done, it is also what is to be done.

The central concern of moral philosophy, then, has always been the double task (1) of meta-ethics, of analyzing the meaning and nature of this normative moral element in mass action, thought and language, and (2) of normative ethics, of evaluating this element by presenting and appraising criteria for justifying rules and judgments of what is morally right and wrong, good and bad. Because in meta-ethics the logic of normative ethics in its various phases is studied, these two parts of moral philosophy are intimately connected.

Moral philosophers have pursued this double task of meta-ethics in a large variety of ways and with a large variety of emphases, a variety that has two main dimensions—one contained within ethics itself, the other deriving from the ethics to other branches of philosophy, to science, to human experience in general. Although these two dimensions are in some respects distinct, the question of precise or proper relation between them itself reflects important divergences among moral philosophers.

What then is ethics? First, the system of value and custom instantiated in the lives of particular groups of human beings is described as the ethics of these groups. Philosophers may concern themselves with articulating these systems, but this is seen as the task of anthropology.

Second, the term is used to refer to one in particular of these systems, 'morality', which involves notions such as rightness and wrongness, guilt and shame, and so on. A central question here is how best to characterize this system. In a moral system one with a certain function, such as to enable cooperation among individuals, or must it involve certain sentiments, such as those concerned with blame.

Third, 'ethics' can, within this system of morality itself, refer to actual moral principles: 'why did you return the book? It was the only ethical thing to do in the circumstances'.

Finally, ethics is that area of philosophy concerned with the study of ethics in other senses. It is important to remember that philosophical ethics is not independent of other areas of philosophy. The answers to many ethical questions depend on answers to questions in metaphysics and other areas. Furthermore, philosophers have been concerned with establishing links between the ethical sphere of life itself and other spheres viz. art and morality or law and morality etc. Some philosophers have, for philosophical reasons, had doubts about whether philosophy provides anyway the best approach to ethics. And even those who believe philosophy has a contribution to make may suggest that ethical justification must refer outside philosophy to common sense beliefs or real life examples.

A central task of philosophical ethics is to articulate what constitutes ethics or morality. This project is that of meta-ethics. What is it that especially constitutes the moral point of view as opposed to others? Some argue that what is morally required is equivalent to what is required by reason overall, whereas others see morality as just one source of reason. Yet others have suggested that all reasons are self-interested, and that concern for others is ultimately irrational. This has not been seen to be inimical in itself to the notion of morality, however, since a moral system can be seen to benefit its participants.

The moral point of view itself is often spelled out as grounded on a conception of equal respect. But there is some debate about how impartial morality requires us to be. Another set of issues concerns what it is that gives a being moral status, either as an object of moral concern or as an actual moral agent. And how do our understandings of human nature impinge on our conception of morality and moral agency?

Once we have some grip on what ethics is, we can begin to ask questions about moral principles themselves. Moral principles have often been put in terms of what is required by duty, but there has been something of a reaction against this notion. Some have seen it as outdated, depending on a conception of divine law with little relevance to the modem world (Schopenhauer, A.), while others have reacted against it as a result of masculine overemphasis on rules at the cost of empathy and care (feminists). These doubts are related to general concerns about the role principles should play in ethical thought. Situation ethicists suggest that circumstances can lead to the abandonment of any moral principle, particularists arguing that this is because it cannot be assumed that a reason that applies in one case will apply in others.

Duties have been seen also as constituting only a part of morality, allowing for the possibility of heroically going beyond the call of duty. This is a matter of the scope of the notion of duty within morality. There are also issues concerning the scope of moral principles more generally. Does a given moral principle apply everywhere, and at all times, or is morality somehow bounded by space or time? How is the capacity of moral judgment acquired? The view that humans possess a special moral sense or capacity for intuition, often identified with conscience, is still found among contemporary intuitionists, viz. Moore, G.E., Ross W.D. *et al.* Skepticism about the claims of morality, however, remains a common view (Nietzsche, F.).

In recent centuries, a dichotomy has opened up between those who believe that morality is based solely on reason, and those who suggest that some irrational component such as desire or emotion is also involved (Hume, D.). Denial of pure rationalism need not lead to giving up of morality. Much work in the twentieth century was devoted to the question of whether moral judgments were best understood as beliefs (and so candidates for truth and falsity), or as disguised expressions of emotions or commands (Stevenson, C.L.). Can there be moral experts or each person entirely responsible for developing their own morality? These questions have been seen as closely tied to issues concerning moral motivation itself. Moral judgments seem to motivate people, so it is tempting to think that they crucially involve a desire.

Moral principles can be understood as resting on moral values, and the debate continues, about how to characterize these values and about how many evaluative assumptions are required to ground ethical claims. Against the emotivists and others, oral realists have asserted the existence of values, some identifying moral properties with those properties postulated in a fully scientific world-view.

ETHICAL CONCEPTS AND ETHICAL THEORIES

Some philosophical ethics is broad and general, seeking to find general principles or explanations of morality. Much, however, focuses on analysis of notions central to ethics itself. One such notion, which has been the focus of much discussion in recent years, is that of autonomy. The interest in self-governance sits alongside with other issues concerning the self, its moral nature and its ethical relation to others, and the relation of these selves in social context. Other topics discussed include the nature of moral ideals, and the notion of desert and moral responsibility.

The question of what makes a human life good for the persons living in it has been at the heart of ethics since the Greek philosophers enquired into *eudaimonia* ('happiness'). The original meaning of the Greek word *eudaimonia is* thriving, flourishing, well-being and has been accepted in the English vocabulary for happiness. In purely abstract terms, x is a value for A if and only if x is a contribution to A's *eudaimonia.* Notice that it is not because a person *wants* a thing that it is a value for him or her. One can want something desperately yet be disappointed or even damaged when one gets it. Desiring or wanting is necessary to motivate, but it cannot be the source of value. We do not *place* a value on something, we find it valuable, or we are in some other way persuaded of its value, may be our parents told us it was valuable, and thus we value it. We can only value a thing if, for some reason, we believe it to be valuable or worthwhile, and if we do not believe it to be valuable or worthwhile (desirable), then we do not value it. A good definition of 'to value, in this sense, would be "to believe valuable". We may conclude that all the values that determine what course of action we ought to choose contribute to the *eudaimonia* of the chooser.

A philosopher's theory of the good will almost always is closely bound up with their views on other central matters. For example, some of those who put weight on sense experience in our understanding of the world have been tempted by the view that the good consists entirely in a particular kind of experience, pleasure. Others have claimed that there is more to life than mere pleasure, and that the good life consists in fulfilling our complex human nature. Nor have philosophers forgotten 'the bad'.

Moral philosophy, or ethics, has long been at least partly concerned with the advocacy of particular ways of living or acting. Some traditions have now declined (e.g., asceticism); but there are still a large range of views on how we should live. One central modern tradition is that of consequentialism. On this view, as it is usually understood, we are required by morality to bring about the greatest good overall (Teleological Ethics). The nature of any consequentialist view, therefore, depends on its view of the good. The most influential theory has been that the only good is the welfare or happiness of individual human and other animals, which, when combined with consequentialism, is utilitarianism (Bentham J. and Mill J.S.).

It is commonly said that consequentialist views are based on the *good*, rather than on the *right*. Theories based on the right may be described as deontological. The towering figure in the deontological tradition has been the eighteenth century German philosopher, Immanuel Kant. Such theories will claim, for example, that we should keep a promise even if more good overall would come for breaking it, or that there are restrictions on what we can intentionally do in pursuit of the good.

In the second half of the twentieth century there was a reaction against some of the perceived excesses of consequentialist and deontological ethics and a return to the ancient notion of *virtues* (or *Arete*). Work in this area consisted partly in attacks on modern ethics, but also in further elaboration and analyses of the virtues and related concepts such as mercy, charity, forgiveness, *help* beneficence, honor, hope, innocence, love, prudence, self-control, trust, truthfulness, etc.

ETHICS FOR EVERYMAN

In dealing with any social problem, we have to regard it from two points of view: (i) the sociological and (ii) the ethical. Sociology, as you all know is the science which formulates the laws according to which events take place in human society; it states in general that such and such social events are caused by such and such other social events. Ethics, on the other hand, is the science which deals with what is good and what is evil, what is right and what is wrong, what ought to be done and what ought not to be done.

Now it is very easy to show that we must attack any social problem from both these standpoints. All that sociology can tell us is that given certain causes, certain effects will follow, and that therefore if we want those effects we must produce those causes. But that is only half the story. It still remains to be asked whether the effect we want to produce is a good effect, that is, one which is desirable to produce, and if it is, what is the *best* way of producing it. And this, ethics alone can say. Take the example of equality of sexes. It may be that equality of the sexes is a bad thing and not worth having; or it may be that even if good in itself, it leads inevitably to consequences so harmful to society that even the evils of the present inequality are preferable. Now this is introducing the ethical point of view. When we begin to ask whether certain thing is good or evil, harmful or beneficial, desirable or undesirable, our question becomes ethical, and its answer can come, not from sociology, but from ethics. It is clear (though it is seldom clearly realized) that this ethical aspect of a social problem is at least as important as the sociological one, and that neglect of it is bound to result in plans, schemes, and programs which may often be positively harmful.

If what has been said above is correct, then we can find a justification for insisting that not only statesmen, and social reformers, but common men also must possess at least a general idea of the ethical principles. A modern civilized society tends to become a democratic society, and under democracy the responsibilities of every individual become greatly enhanced. Among other things, he has to vote for or against measures which, if taken, will affect more or less seriously his way and conditions of life; and it is essential, before he can vote for or against them, that he should be able to satisfy himself that they are on the whole either beneficial or harmful.

We as rational beings ought to see that our actions are as far as possible right and not wrong. Now it is hardly possible to do this without knowledge of what constitutes the rightness or wrongness of an action. Of course, it does not follow that if a man knew what is right and what is wrong, he would always choose the former and avoid the latter. But it can be safely said that given a desire on the part of men to be good, they are more likely to succeed if they know what is good than if they do not.

The idea of 'good' is the most fundamental of all ideas with which ethics has to deal with. Now, one may ask what is the definition of 'good'? Someone will answer: "Good is good, and there is nothing more to be said about it". This is so because 'good' is simple and cannot be defined. It is an *ultimate* principle. None of the definitions of 'good' suggested by philosophers are real definitions at all. The basic principle to be remembered here is that the *definiendum* (or the names to be defined) and the *definiens* (or the definition given) mean the *same* thing; that is, they refer to the same object.

Let us examine some of the definitions. John Stuart Mill suggested that "what is pleasant (desired) is good (desirable)". Now the question arises: "Is everything that is pleasant good?" The answer would be no. It follows that 'pleasant' and 'good' are different things, and, therefore, the former cannot be treated as the definition of the latter. Some theologians will define 'good' as "what is the will of God". Does God will good always? We may ask the same question to the theologians which Socrates asked Euthyphron who held the similar doctrine: "Does God will a thing because it is good or does that thing becomes good because He wills it?" This question clearly proves that the two notions of "good" and " being willed by God" are entirely different and cannot be regarded as the *definiendum* and *definiens.* A third expression, which often appears to be treated as the definition of 'good', is that used by those writers on Ethics who have their theories on the doctrine of Evolution. Herbert Spencer, for example, says in his *Data of Ethics* "conduct gains ethical sanction as the activities, becoming less and less militant, and are furthered by co-operation and mutual aid". In short, more evolved conduct is *better* conduct: Survival in evolution is good. Now it may be that whatever survives in the course of evolution is also always good. However, in order to accept survival as a value, and that it may be regarded as the definition of 'good', it is necessary that the two should be identical. Can we say that the two are identical? It is clear that we cannot. Similarly we can also reject those definitions which suggest 'self-realization', 'living according to Nature', and similar other things as the correct definitions of 'good'. Indeed it is indefinable because it is an *ultimate* principle and not simply a means to an end.

Now, the question arises as to what is 'good'? One of the

most famous ethical theories has been the one called 'Hedonism', which held that pleasure is the only good. Its briefest and the best expression is to be found in the classic phrase of Jeremy Bentham: "the greatest happiness of the greatest number", which, he held, is the ideal of human endeavor. But this theory has rarely found favor with majority of moralists, and Hedonism has generally been supposed to be a theory of shallow thinkers who do not know much about morality. The question of pleasure thus has occupied an important position in ethical discussions, and I think it will be worthwhile to state clearly the place of pleasure in moral life. The word 'pleasure' covers all agreeable feelings or states of consciousness. It includes not only the pleasures of the body but also others which are not bodily, but may be called mental pleasures like those of aesthetic appreciation of the beauty in color or sound and even the feeling of satisfaction that comes to us from the doing of our duty.

I think that it is perfectly clear that the pleasure is intrinsically good; but of course when we say this we consider pleasure by itself, for it will be remembered that whether a thing is good in itself can only be found if we isolate it completely from everything else, that is, from things along with which it may enter into organic wholes or things to which it may give rise. When we so isolate pleasure, we find that it is valuable for its own sake, that it is better that it should exist than that it should not exist. It cannot then be doubted that pleasure is good in itself.

Pleasure by itself is certainly intrinsically good. But we rarely meet it alone. Generally it is to be met with as part of wholes, and as part of wholes it does not always have a good effect on those wholes. In some wholes, e.g., those of aesthetic appreciation and personal affections, pleasure enhances the goodness of the whole; whereas in some other wholes, e.g. those in which there is love or admiration or enjoyment of what is ugly or evil, pleasure *heightens the badness* of the whole. For this reason, pleasure is to be avoided in the latter kind of cases.

Now anybody who knows what is meant by 'good' becomes acquainted sooner or later with another notion, which seems to be equally simple and indefinable; viz., the notion of 'ought'. I do not think that 'ought' can be defined. We may not always agree as to *what* we ought to do; but we are all agreed that we *ought* to do something. You may try to find out for yourself whether 'ought' is not a simple notion as 'good'. Since it is a simple notion, it is therefore indefinable.

The general principle of conduct should be "The greatest amount of good possible ought to be created", though it cannot be proved as it is an *ultimate* principle and is self-evident. From this principle and the two notions of 'good" and 'ought' can be derived all the rest of the notions of ethics, such as 'right', 'wrong', etc. It should be noted that 'right' and 'wrong' are the adjectives of actions alone, and not of things. A thing is either good or bad, but neither right nor wrong; in like manner, an action is either right or wrong, but neither good nor bad. It is true that we often talk of good actions and bad actions; but in such cases we mean merely actions which produce good results and those which produce bad results.

'Right' means 'what we are morally bound to do' viz. that action which will cause more good to exist in the universe than any other alternative possible under the circumstances. Another name for a right action is 'duty'. 'Wrong' means' what ought not to be done' or what is morally forbidden', viz. that action which will cause *less* good than it is possible to create in the circumstances.

Right action has been defined here as that action which produces a greater balance of good over evil than any other action possible under any given circumstances. Now in judging the rightness or wrongness of an action must be reckoned not merely the consequences of the action, but also the action itself, and even the agent's intention or motive for doing it. For the action itself may possess either positive or negative intrinsic value; and even if it does not possess any intrinsic value, still the principle of organic wholes would forbid us to suppose that it does not add to or subtract from the value of the whole of which it may form a part. The same can be said of the motive or intention. It may have positive or negative value; and even if it did not have this, still it may be capable of enhancing or detracting from the value of the whole of which it may form a part. Further, the intention of the agent may have its own effects, at any rate upon the character of the agent. Now there is no reason why these things should be excluded from the consideration of the morality of action; on the other hand, there is every reason why they should be included. And let there be no mistake about what is meant by the 'results' of an action. These include not merely the immediate effects of the acts in question, but also the effects of those effects, and so on without end. The results whose intrinsic value is to be computed are absolutely *all* the results of the actions in question. Rightness or the wrongness of an action depends not on the intention merely, nor on the intention plus the action, but on these two and the whole chain of results, which follow from them.

No man or woman may hope to be moral, that is, to do right action, unless he or she possesses some knowledge of the nature of universe, of human society, and of the principles of ethics. For calculation of the value of the results of our action, such as is possible for us mortals, is only possible on the basis of such knowledge. Consequently, those poets, moralists, philosophers, and politicians who praise the simplicity and innocence of children and rustics and pretend that no great knowledge is required in order to live a good life, may be dismissed as quite mistaken.

Now, we turn to another important question. Which things are good as *means*? It is important to remember in this connection that the things, which are good in themselves, may be good as means, and that even things which are evil in themselves may be *good* as means. That is to say, intrinsic goods, besides being good in themselves, may be further productive of intrinsic goods; and intrinsic evils, though evil in themselves, may be used to produce intrinsically good effects or to avoid intrinsically evil ones. For example, punishment considered by itself, is evil since it causes pain, but it may be inflicted on men in order to *prevent* future crimes by deterring prospective wrong-doers and to *reform* the present ones. But besides these intrinsically good and bad things, *almost anything may be productive of good results.* It is therefore impossible to make an exhaustive list of things, which are good as means. However, there are a few things that are of supreme importance as means of producing good. Of these I shall single out four here, viz., (i) Knowledge, (ii) Freedom, (iii) Equality, and (iv) Good Governance.

(i) Whether knowledge by itself has great intrinsic value may be doubted. Certainly the mere possession of information on one or more subjects is not particularly valuable *in itself*. However, the pursuit of knowledge, the patient and difficult struggle with nature to compel her to disclose her secrets, does appear to be one of the most valuable things known to us. Though mere possession of information on a large number of subjects is hardly of any value in itself, still considered as a means to good knowledge has very great value. This is so, not merely because by means of knowledge men can secure their ends better than brutes or ignorant savages, but also for another important reason. This reason is that without some knowledge of the relevant spheres of nature and human society computation of the value of the likely results (on which alone the decision as to which action is comparatively right can be based) is impossible. Thus, knowledge is necessary for making a correct decision as to which action has to be chosen. It is certainly one of the proper functions of the state to help them in this task.

(ii) As in the case of knowledge, it may be doubted whether freedom has much intrinsic value. But that it has some intrinsic value seems probable. An action never has any intrinsic value (though it may cause intrinsic value) unless a person out of free choice does it, that is, not because he is compelled to do it, but because he voluntarily chooses it for its good effects. In fact, unless an action is voluntary, we cannot call it right or wrong. If a man refrains from stealing when it is perfectly possible for him to do so with impunity, then his action certainly appears to have some intrinsic value, whereas if he refrains from stealing merely because he is too well watched to do it, his action would have no moral value at all. This point has great significance in the treatment of certain personal relations. It is the very essence of love or friendship that the emotions must be freely given and not extorted; where there is any coercion of any kind, there cannot be any love.

But besides being good in itself, freedom has great value as a means to the production of great intrinsic goods and prevention of great evils. All sentient creatures seem endowed with a measure of craving for independence, so that whenever it is thwarted they experience pain; and this pain is greater in proportion as an animal is more mentally developed. In the case of man the unhappiness caused by slavery knows no bounds. This immense misery can be removed only by means of freedom. But besides this, freedom is further a pre-condition of the highest achievements of human mind in knowledge, art, and social life. No discovery in science was ever made by a slave nor did any bondman create a work of art. Without freedom it seems impossible that our civilization could have ever been built.

(iii) Another thing, which is extremely valuable as a means, is equality. It seems pretty clear that in itself equality is not worth much; but as a constituent in valuable organic wholes and also as a means of creating valuable things its value is very great. Our personal relations as friends or husband and wife or father and child must be based upon equality and freedom in order to be valuable. It is also important for another reason. Equal opportunity to all for the development of their capacities is essential if we want the maximum good to be produced by men. The majority of children never get the chance of a civilized life, which means that the majority of the population today is prevented from contributing their share of good to the community.

(iv) It is clear that the creation and accumulation of great goods is impossible in an atmosphere of general insecurity, where life and property are in constant danger of destruction. To make a good life possible therefore it is necessary to formulate rules of conduct and establish institutions, which will secure safety for life, property and freedom, and to back these rules by sanctions of some powerful authority. Such authority in the modern world is the state. Hence both the existence of a good state and the obedience of its rules are essential pre-conditions of the production of any great goods; and consequently it is our duty to bring such a State into existence where it does not exist and to obey its rules where it does. Forced morality does not of course have any value *in itself*;

for an action to be valuable in itself must be done voluntarily and not out of necessity. But though not good in itself, this forced morality is immensely valuable as a means owing to its capacity for preventing great evils.

ETHICS AND HUMAN WELL-BEING

The problem which morality is supposed to solve, which is the central problem for ethics, is how to reconcile the unavoidable separateness of persons with their inherently social nature and circumstances. Every moral outlook and every moral theory is an attempt to solve this problem. Hard or tough egoistic individualism says you should exploit other people as much as you can for your own advantage. But if everyone adopted this view (and as a moral view it must be universalizable), everyone would be in perpetual adversarial conflict with everyone else. It would not be a very happy situation.

The Hobbsian Contractarian view, which is also egoistic, says it is too dangerous to try for the best we could have for ourselves, which would be to dominate and exploit everybody. Therefore, we would settle for the second best and agree with others to limit our conduct in such a way that we do not live in perpetual fear of one another. This is a much better situation. Justice and right have entered the picture, but we are still concerned with our own individual selves. There is no concern for the common good in its own right. The trouble with this view is that I have the reason to believe I can violate the contract and get away with it, there is *no* reason why I should not do just that. If there is concern for justice only in so far as it profits *me,* there is no concern for justice itself.

The Kantian view is non-egoistic but still individualistic. I must not do what I cannot will that others do whenever they feel like it. I must be aware of the reality of others. But people are still conceived as a collection of individuals and not as a community. This view is not altruistic but *universalist.* But there is also a *communal* reason for obeying the categorical imperative, for it helps to create the kind of social atmosphere in which people can live richer and more fulfilling lives. In other words, it is a contribution to the common good.

Consequentialist utilitarianism is not the solution because it sees deontic morality as a *complete and general guide to conduct*, an ethics of *general prescription*, when in fact we know that deontic morality is an ethics of *limitation* based on the idea of law. Consequentialist utilitarianism is also not altruistic but universalist. It is also individualistic, seeing only an aggregate of persons rather than a community. Communitarianism sees the individual not as alone, unattached, and isolated, but sees his or her social relations and membership in the community as an essential part of himself or herself. This is a step in the right direction, but unfortunately communitarians see the individual's good as partly constituted by existing institutions and social relations whatever they may be. The question of what constitutes a good community is not asked. Communitarianism then seems to be a kind of cultural relativism in disguise.

Collectivism is the view that personal interests should be sacrificed to the general good, generally seen as represented by the state. But this ignores the separateness of persons and their need to lead their own lives. It is out of accord with human nature. If the common good, for which morality exists, is a necessary part of the good life for each individual, the opposition between individualism and collectivism is overcome. It is true that our social relations are real, and part of ourselves, but that good social relations require a community in which both the virtues and deontic morality are encouraged and supported. Moral goodness is necessary for, and partly constitutes, the good community.

If value external to practices is pursued to the detriment of values internal to practices, the result is adversarial competition and a loss of important goods. External values should be the reward of internal values and should not be pursued independently of them. If internal values are pursued for their own sake, not only will more things of real value be produced, but this will tend to encourage the virtues and discourage bad character and moral wrongdoing. There is nothing wrong with material goods if they enhance our lives. Materialism in the bad sense is (a) greed, which is *moral vice*; and (b) thinking of material goods as the only value in life. Good work in producing valuable goods and services is fulfilling to the spirit, no matter how material these goods and services may be. Thus the opposition between the material and the spiritual is overcome.

Bond (1996, pp. 228–31) has developed a moral theory of *communalism:* (a) to indicate that it is not individualistic; and (b) to distinguish it from communitarianism and collectivism. It has been argued (1) that there is a morality valid for all humanity (a universal and objective morality grounded in practical reason); (2) that the ultimate source of all value, including moral value, is *eudaimonia* (thriving, flourishing, well-being, happiness), both communal and personal (the former being necessary for the latter); (3) that the aretic and the deontic are separate but necessary constituents of a single morality; (4) that the theory of communalism, by showing the tie between moral goodness and the common good, *does* reconcile the separateness of persons with their inherently social nature; and (5) that being morally good is neither egoistic nor altruistic, but overcomes this opposition altogether.

Communalism, thus, will be able to solve the problem of separateness of persons with their inherently social nature and that the well-being of humanity as a whole can be achieved. He thinks that a morality valid for all humanity (a universal and objective morality grounded in practical reason) is possible, as the ultimate source of all value, including moral value, is *eudaimonia* (thriving, flourishing, well-being, happiness), both communal and personal, the former being necessary for the latter. He argues that the acetic and deontic are separate but necessary constituents of a single morality. The theory of communalism by showing the tie between goodness and the common good, said to be a necessary ingredient of the happiness of each individual, does reconcile the separateness of persons with their inherently social nature. Being morally good is neither egoistic nor altruistic; moral goodness overcomes the unfortunate dichotomy. He goes on to say: "what is morally good is whatever is in conduct and character that brings people together in amity and goodwill, while allowing them to live fulfilling and self-directed individual lives; what is morally evil is whatever is in conduct and character that divides people and sets them against one another, while hindering them from living rich and fulfilling self-directed individual lives. And if this is so ... moral goodness does not require selflessness, self-denial, or self-sacrifice. Because the common good is an essential ingredient of the good of each and every individual, making it desirable that we act for its sake, the supposed opposition between egoism and altruism has been overcome. Our overall conclusion is that the morally good life, properly understood, is the best life for each and all".

The ethical and moral concepts in Hellenism and Hinduism vary immensely. This is because of the different world-views. The concepts of 'goodness', 'morality', and 'ethical behavior' are quite different in both of these civilizations. In Hellenism the good of the State and its rulers was the primary concern, while in India, universal good and welfare of all was the primary concern (*sarve bhavantu sukhinah sarve santu niramayah*).

CHAPTER 6

In Retrospect

Hellenism and Hinduism are basically responsible for the growth of the basic tenets of the Occidental and Oriental cultures, respectively. Yet, both the religions are not properly understood because their nature and the basic forms have not been properly understood or analyzed. Since Hellenism and Hinduism represent the real spirit and values of the two different world-views of the Indo-European people living in two extremes of the geographical horizons of the Indo-European world, and that they have a long tradition and history much of which still survive in their cultures, it has been decided to investigate the origins and development of these two great traditions in order to see why the spirit of Hellenism is lost in the country of its birth whereas the spirit of Hinduism still exists in India.

It is true that in the domain of plastic arts, Greece owed nothing to India with which she made acquaintance very late, but it is equally true that in the field of language, religion, and mythology it owed much to India. We have already seen that there are four distinct historical phases of Greek culture: (1) before Alexander, the classical phase as a national culture; (2) after Alexander, Hellenism as a cosmopolitan secular culture; (3) later Hellenism as a pagan religious culture; and (4) Byzantinism as a Greek Christian culture. The transition from the first to the second phase is for the most part explained as an autonomous Greek development. In the second phase (300 BC–first century AD) the Greek spirit was represented by the great rival schools of philosophy, the Academy, the Epicureans, and above all the Stoics, while at the same time the Greek-oriental synthesis was progressing. The transition from the third phase, the turning to religion of ancient civilizations as a whole and of the Greek mind with it, was the work of profoundly un-Greek forces which, originating in the East, entered history as new factors. Between the rule of Hellenistic secular and the final defensive position of the late Hellenism turned religious lie three centuries of revolutionary spiritual movements which effected this transformation, among which the gnostic movement occupies a prominent place.

We are concerned here only with the first phase in which the real national Greek spirit (Hellenism) came into existence. The roots of Hellenism can at the best be traced back to c. 1900 BC, the beginning of the Middle Helladic Period on the Mainland Greece, although most of the scholars do not agree with this date. They are of the opinion that the date could be only in about 1300 BC, the date of the tablets from Pylos bearing the inscriptions in Linear B script. We have also seen that all the linguists, archaeologists, and historians connect the incoming of the Greeks with a branch of the Indo-European from somewhere outside Greece. They came with sophisticated form of beaurocratic government. They knew fort building and besides possessing sea faring expertise were rank fighters with deadly weapons in their arms. They were not simply agrarian people moving with livestock on horseback as was hitherto supposed. They settled first on the Mainland Greece and destroyed the great Minoan Civilization of Crete, from where we have got the inscriptions (Phaistos Disc) in Linear A, which though still undeciphered, may have belonged to original non-Indo-European inhabitants of the island. Many non-Greek words in the vocabulary of the Greek language may be their gift.

In our study of the Indo-European languages we have seen that the earliest date of the Rigveda is still not clear, yet it could be placed anywhere between 3000 and 5000 BC. The finding of a large number of names identical to Puranic characters on the Sumerian tablets, well dated in between 2600 BC and 3600 BC, proves the above date. Moreover, many of the cosmogonical and cosmological representations on the antiquities of the 'Old Europe', dated between the 5th and the 4th millennium BC, carry the mythological narration of cosmogony of the *Rigveda.* So far as the Greek cosmogonical and cosmological narration is concerned we have seen that its cosmogony was certainly too vague, carrying its past memories in a highly confused manner. However, in cherishing a common theory of cosmogony, the theory of advent of gods from a pair of parents, the recognition of variety of gods associated with natural phenomena, along with the mystic ideology of the existence of soul and its reincarnation, common both to India and Greece are such strong traits for which one may search in vain elsewhere except in the Vedic Aryans.

As far as the philosophers of the classical Greek period are concerned, they have not given us anything new that was not known to the Vedic seers. In the field of philosophical discussions about man and its relationship with cosmos, there is much in common between the two great cultures. However, the antiquity of the Indo-Aryan culture is much more than the Hellenic culture. As such, it seems that during the classical phase when Greece came into contact with the Indian culture, her old memory revived about the transcendental thinking of the Vedic seers, for example, Plato's concept that the soul in the body is as a sailor in the ship or that each distinct mode of being has an invariable nature which determines its basic tendencies (cf. *Guna* and *karma* in *Bhagavadgita*). Scholarly opinion confirms the view that whatever Pythagoras and Empedocles taught to men in their own land was borrowed and learnt by them on the Indian subcontinent. The doctrine of transmigration of souls was indigenous to India and was brought to Greece by Pythagoras. Plato also believed in it. The source of Greek mysticism and philosophy seems to be India from where we get all the parallels in earlier times.

Rational wisdom is the very heart and core of Greek thought. This is the Greek view of man *par excellence.* Reason is the highest cognitive power, capable of grasping the immobile structures of nature. The aim of moral training, is the acquisition of firm rational habits, or virtues, which fall into two major groups, the intellectual and the moral. The intellectual virtues enable us to understand being as it is. There are two basic genera of moral virtue: justice, which concerns the rational direction of our overt, social acts; and passional virtue, which concerns the control of our own subjective passion. The latter is a necessary condition for the former, which has no mean.

The concept of justice of Greek thinkers is also very much alike the Indian thought. For them, to act justly is to render to each thing and to each person, including ourselves, what is due to it by nature. Justice is divided into three species. First of all, there is social justice in the broad Platonic sense of rendering to each distinct nature what is due, as this could be understood by reason. Besides this, Aristotle distinguishes two other specific types of justice. The first is distributive justice, an equal sharing of common goods and common burdens by all individuals alike, or in proportion to real merit. The second is the commutative justice of exchange, where absolute equality should rule.

These Greek thoughts had great influence on the religious traditions of the Hellenistic and Roman periods. We find the Greek view of man in the Mohammedan and Christian thoughts also. I have discussed in detail the western concept of justice in general and social justice in particular. The conclusion of the entire discussion is that without being spiritual, or having some sort of faith in the supernatural, merely rational thinking of the material world cannot bring social justice or human well-being.

Classical scholars have been talking of only one "golden age" in Greece during the Periclean period. However, now the classical archaeologists working in Greece have traced two other "golden age" in the pre-classical period—the New-Palace Period of Minoan Crete and the culminating phase of the Mycenean period on the mainland. The Minoan civilization, eastern in character, was not only the finest achievement of the Aegean Bronze Age, but also the first advanced civilization to flourish on European soil. From its remote position in the extreme southwest corner of the continent, the Minoan civilization shone out brilliantly over both the Aegean and the mainland. Before its own light dimmed, it succeeded in illuminating the path ahead which the more primitive peoples of the Helladic Greece could follow, and in providing, through its own achievements, the spark of inspiration they needed to create their own new civilization. However, many of the scholars do not agree with this proposition. They are of the view that the Mycenean civilization is the product of the mainland, though certain cultural elements, particularly in the field of art and architecture, sculpture, and painting, they certainly borrowed from Crete; but their language and pottery styles were quite different from them.

The Mycenean civilization did in fact continue along the path paved by its predecessors up to the end of the Bronze Age, but it had a vigor and spirit of its own and a more decisive influence on later Greek history, since its own character determined to a large extent the character of Greek civilization in the subsequent Archaic period, a period reflected in the epics of Homer.

The disintegration of the Mycenean State did not bring about the end of the Mycenean civilization. Nor did the eventual destruction of this civilization wipe out all its achievements. To some degree at least, the Creto-Mycenean heritage survived and was handed down through subsequent generations. This happened at a critical turning point in history: the transition from the Bronze Age to the Iron Age. The change in culture took place at approximately the same period throughout the whole of the Eastern Mediterranean. The changes, which came about during this period in the whole of the surrounding areas had important results in Greece, now emerging from the obscure period, called the Greek "Middle Ages". The term is misleading, but it does reflect on our present ignorance of this new critical phase. Most of the recent researches seek to match the information given in the epic poems with the archaeological evidence. We can certainly form an idea and speculate about its character and trace the path of the Creto-Mycenean heritage in the Classical Hellenic Civilization. It is now a well-established fact that in spite of all the upheavals of the "Dark Ages", there was no break between the Mycenean and post-Mycenean world. What exactly was the heritage and how was it handed down? How extensive was it and how significant from a historical point of view? The answer to these questions could be found in the study of the Mycenean and post-Mycenean civilizations and in the study of the ethnic and linguistic groups in prehistoric Greece.

There is plenty of evidence, gathered both recently and in the past, to show that elements of the Mycenean civilization either survived into or reappeared in historical times; the idea of the city-state, the megaron-shaped plan of the Greek temple, the nuclei of the epics, the language of the Greeks. For all the excellent work being done in this broad field of research, the subject has not by any means been exhausted. Indeed, new fields of study have opened up especially after the decipherment of the Mycenean script, linear B. Leaving on one side all other manifestations of culture, we may observe that the ethical value of the Mycenean alone played a decisive role in shaping the culture of historical Greece.

The heritage from the heroic age influenced not only the cults and myths, but also the entire spiritual life and education of the Greeks in historical times. The idea of national unity had its roots in the heroic age, and again it was in this period that the Greeks turned whatever a treaty or alliance needed to be justified historically. It was the common tradition more than a common language or country, which united the Greek race. The survival and transmitting of this tradition would naturally have been impossible had there been no ethnic continuity in Greece. The Mycenean at the end of the Mycenean period—the people who had handed down this tradition—were basically Indo-European people. But they were also Greek. It was precisely this mixing of tribes and cultures, which has produced the Mycenean "miracle". Also, there are no doubts that some fairly substantial remnants of the Mycenean population remained. They were subdued or transferred where they could do no harm. Some were sent to distant coasts or islands, such as Cyprus, where there is no doubt that they had an influence on later developments. This is shown by the fact that the greatest cultural progress in historical times was achieved in Attica, a region not settled by the newly arrived Greeks.

It is a truism that the creative spirit of Crete inspired the Helladic world. And we can appreciate how much poorer the Mycenean civilization would have been without the influence of the Minoan by noting the much lower level of civilization achieved by other European countries in the Bronze Age.

The old belief that there was a gulf between the prehistoric and historical times was supported by the theory that the "northerner" tribe descended into Greece in c. 1100 BC bringing the Olympian gods and the Greek spirit to the "pre-Hellenic world" has now been abandoned, for Greek history no longer begins with the coming of the Dorians. The new age, which begins at the dawn of historical times, is not completely cut off from the past. More and more evidence of Mycenean influence is coming to light all the time. And it is certain that the ethnic continuity of the Greeks from the beginning of the second millennium BC will be established, whether or not the present interpretation of the Mycenean texts continues to be accepted.

We now know that the Myceneans are part of the Hellenic World and tradition, consequently, the heritage they bequeathed to later generations must have played an important role in forming the civilizations of both Archaic and Classical Greece. Nonetheless it demonstrates the inherent strength of the Greek people and their astonishing power of survival; they still exist and flourish today, retaining their distinctive character, their language, and their exclusiveness along with their cohesiveness, despite intense individualism. Apart possibly from the Indian and, probably Chinese, there are few, if any, other comparable peoples in their tenacity to endure. In their long history they have at least three times blossomed out into world leadership in culture: in the Late Mycenaean Age, in the Classical period, and in the heyday of the Byzantine Empire.

The same story is true of the Indian civilization. We know that Northern India at the time of the expansion of Greater Greece, that is to say, when Alexander entered the vestibule of the gates of India, had attained a high degree of civilization, which must have been the product of evolution continued through many centuries. Fortunately, we now know that the great Indian civilization had its roots deep in antiquity, some seven to eight thousand years ago, and its flowering in the third millennium BC. It still lives on, not as a fugitive but as a vital organ of our socio-cultural fabric. In contrast, when we look round the world we are surprised by the fact that the Egyptian and Mesopotamian civilizations that flourished alongside the Indian civilization have all disappeared, leaving hardly any trace behind. The reason lies in the Indian psyche which has indeed been pondering over this great cultural phenomenon of 'livingness'. There was something in our civilization which has withstood the onslaught of invaders and time. 'It was its inherent strength. Doubtless it lies in the liberal character of the Indian civilization, which allows for cross-fertilization with other cultures, without losing its own identity. Even time *(kala)*, the great devourer, has stood testimony to the fact that the deep foundations of Indian culture could not be shaken either by internal upheavals, or by the infiltrating extra-territorial cultural waves' (Lal, 2002, p. 136).

To sum up, the Greek and Indian civilizations have many traits in common, viz. language, comogonical and mystical thinking, concept of man and humanism, theory of justice, ethics, and morality. However, the traditional original thinking still continues in Hinduism but not in Hellenism. It is simply because of the fact that it was highjacked by those who overran Greece after the death of Alexander the Great and we can only trace its elements in the amalgam of the Greek and Eastern thoughts which we find in the Hellenistic period. Hellenism was lost in the land of its birth completely with the coming up of the Roman and Byzantine powers.

Bibliography

Abraham H. Maslow, 1953: *Man's Search for Himself,* New York.

Adrados, F.R., 1990: "The archaic structure of Hittite: the crux of the problem" In: *Journal of Indo-European Studies* 10, pp. 1–35.

Agnes Heller, 1996: *An Ethics of Personality,* Oxford-Basil, Blackwell.

Agrawal, V. S., 1963: *Matsya Purana: A Study,* Varanasi, All India Kashiraj Institute.

Akhtar, Jamna Das, 1978-79: 'Indo-Aryan rulers of Ancient Western Asia and their Documents', In *Puratattva,* No. 10, pp. 66–69.

Albright, W.G., 1949: *Archaeology of Palestine.*

Albright, F.E., 1966: *Archaeology, "Historical Analogy" and Early Biblical Tradition,* Balton Rouge, Louisiana State University Press.

Alisdair, Macintyre, 1988: *Whose Justice? Which Reality?*, London, Gerald Duckworth & Coy. Ltd.

Alisdair, Macintyre, 1998: *A Short History of Ethics: A History of Moral Philosophy from Homeric Age to the Twentieth Century*, 2nd edn., London, Routledge.

Allchin, B. & R., 1982: *The Rise of Civilization in India and Pakistan*, London, Cambridge University Press.

Ammarman and Cavalli-Sforza, L.L., 1973: "A population model for the diffusion of early framing in Europe." In C. Renfrew (ed.) *The Explanation of Culture Change, Models in Prehistory*, London, Duckworth, pp. 343–58.

Ammarman and Cavalli-Sforza, L.L., 1991: "Genes, People and Language." In *Scientific American*, 265, pp. 71–78.

Anthony Flew, 1979: *A Dictionary of Philosophy*, London, Pan Books.

Anthony, D.W. & B. Wales, 1988: Review of C. Renfrew, *Archaeology and Language, Current Anthropology* 29:441–5.

Apte, V.S., 1984: *Sanskrit Hindi Dictionary*, Delhi, Motilal Banarasidas.

Aristotle, 1980: *Nicomachean Ethics,* excerpts in Sterba James (ed.) *Justice: Alternative Political Perspectives,* Wadsworth.

Arora, U.P., 1981: *Motifs in Indian Mythology: Their Greek and other Parallels,* New Delhi, Munshiram Manoharlal.

Arora, U.P., 1996: *Greeks on India,* Bareilly, ISGARS Publications.

Arora, U.P., 1997: *India and the Hellenistic World, Bareilly,* ISGARS Publications.

Arturo Speziale, 1987: *Ethical and Religious Values of Ancient India: 3000 BC - 650 AD,* Sujan Publications, Calcutta.

Asko Parpola, 1985: The Sky-garment: A study of the Harappan Religion and its relation to the Mesopotamian and Later Indian Religions, In *Studia Orientalia*-57, Helsinki, Finnish Oriental Society.

Asko Parpola, 1994: *Deciphering the Indus Script,* Cambridge.

Asko Parpola, A.S. Koskenniemi, S. Parpola and P. Aalto, 1969: *Decipherment of the Proto-Dravidian Indus Script: A First Announcement.* Copenhagen.

Ayer, A.J. (ed.), 1968: *The Humanistic Outlook,* London.

Bacon Edward (ud.): *Vanished Civilization,* p. 227.

Banerjee, G.N., 1990: *India as known to the Ancient World*, New Delhi (First Published in 1921).

Banerjee, G.N., 1995: *Hellenism in Ancient India,* New Delhi, Mittal Publications (First Published in London in 1920).

Barry, B., 1989: *Theories of Justice*, Berkeley, University of California Press.

Basak, R.G., 1959: *Asokan Inscriptions,* Delhi.

Basham, A.L., 1990, *Origins and Development of Classical Hinduism, Delhi,* Oxford University Press.

Baxi, Upendra (ed.), 1987: *The Right to be Human*, New Delhi.

Benveniste, E., 1973: *The Indo-European Language and Society,* Florida, Coral Gables.

Berger, Peter L., 1976: *Pyramids of Sacrifice: Political Ethics and Social Change,* Allen Lane, London.

Bhattacharya, Buddhadeva, 1969: *Evolution of the Political Philosophy of Gandhi*, Calcutta-Book House, Calcutta.

Bhattacharya, N.N., 1970: *History of Indian Cosmogonical Ideas,* New Delhi, Munshiram Manoharlal.

Bhattacharya, P.B., 1980: The Indus Valley Civilization – An Aryan Culture, in *Puratattva-11,* Indian Archaeological Society, New Delhi, pp. 140–45.

Bhattacharya, N.N., (ed.) 1998: *Encyclopedia of Ancient Indian Culture,* New Delhi, Manohar Publishers.

Bilabel, 1927: *Geschichte Vorderasiens,* I, 1927, pp. 270 ff.

Bittel, Kurt, 1975: *Guide to Boghazkoy,* Ankara, Turkey.

Blackburn, Simon, 1994: *The Oxford Dictionary of Philosophy,* Oxford University Press, New York.

Blackham, H.J., 1968: *Humanism,* Penguin Books.

Blegen, Carl W., 1928: *Zygouries: A Prehistoric Settlement in the Valley of Cleonae,* Cambridge, Mass.

Bloomfield, L., 1906: In *American Journal of Philology,* xxv, p. 8.

Bond, E. J., 1996: *Ethics and Human Well-being: an Introduction to Moral Philosophy,* Cambridge, Blackwell.

Bongard-Levin, G.M., 1971: Studies in Ancient India and Central Asia, In *Indian Studies: Past and Present-3,* Calcutta.

Bongard-Levin, G.M., 1980: *The Origin of Aryans,* Arnold-Heinemann, New Delhi.

Bongard-Levin, G.M., 1986: *A Complex Study of Ancient India: A Multi-disciplinary Approach,* Delhi, Ajanta Publications (Part III: Problems of Cultural Development: Ancient India and World Civilization, Chapter 8 and 9 on Ancient India and Graeco-Roman world).

Bopp F., 1816: *Uber das conjugations system der Sanskrit sprache in Vergleichung mit jenem der griechischen, lateinischen, persischen and germanischen Sprache,* Frankfurt am Main, Andrea.

Bopp F., 1839: *Die Celtischen Sprachen in ihrem Verhaltnisse zum Sanskrit, Zend, Griechischen, Lateinschen, Germanischen, Litanischen and Siawischen,* Berlin.

Bosch-Gimpera P., 1960: *EI Problema Indoeuropeo, Mexico,* Direction General de Publicaciones.

Bosch-Gimpera P., 1961: *Les Indo-Europeans,* Paris, Payot.

Brian Barry, 1989: *Theories of Justice,* University of California Press, Berkeley.

Brown, W. Norman, 1965: Theories of Creation the RigVeda, in *Journal of American Oriental Society* 85, pp. 23–24.

Bruce A. Ackerman, 1980: *Social Justice in the Liberal State,* Yale University Press, New Haven and London.

Brunswig, R.H., 1975: In *East and West,* New Series, 1-2, March, pp. 112, 114.

Buck, C.D., 1949: *Dictionary of Selected Synonyms in the Principal Indo-European Languages,* Chicago.

Buddha Prakash, 1964: *India and the World,* Hoshiarpur, Vivekanand Vedic Research Institute.

Burkert, Walter, 1985: *Greek Religion* (trans. By John Raffan), Harvard University Press, Cambridge, Mass.

Burrow, T., 1955: *The Sanskrit Language,* London, pp. 27–29
Bynon, Theodra, 1997: *Historical Linguistics,* Cambridge.
Campbell, E.F., 1964: *The Chronology of Amarna Letters,* p. 102.
Campbell, et al. (eds), 1986: *Human Rights: From Rhetoric to Reality,* Blackwell, London.
Cardona, George, et al. (eds.) 1970: *Indo-European and Indo-Europeans,* University of Pennsylvania, Philadelphia.
Carter, Stephen L., 1994: *The Culture of Disbelief,* Anchor Books, New York.
Cassirer, E., 1944: *An Essay on Man: An Introduction to a Philosophy of Human Culture*, New Haven, Yale University Press.
Cassirer, E., 1963: *The Individual and the Cosmos in the Renaissance Philosophy* (Trans. By Mario Domandi), Oxford, Basil Blackwell.
Cassirer, E., 1965: *The Philosophy of Symbolic Forms*, Trans. By C.W. Hendel, New Haven, CT: Yale University Press.
Cavalli-Sforza, L.L., 1973: "A population model for the diffusion of early farming in Europe". In C. Renfrew (ed.) *The Explanation of Culture Change, Models in Prehistory*, London, Duckworth, pp. 343–58.
Cavalli-Sforza, L.L., 1991: "Genes, People and Language". In *Scientific American*, 265, pp. 71–78.
Cavalli-Sforza, L.L., 1994: *The History and Geography of Human Genes*, Princeton University, Princeton.
Cavalli-Sforza, L.L., 2000: *Genes People and Languages,* North Point Press.
Cavalli-Sforza, L.L., Alberto Piazza, Paolo Minozzi, and Joanna Mountain, 1988: "Reconstruction of Human Evolution: Bringing Together Genetic, Archaeological and Linguistic Data", *Proceedings of the National Academy of Sciences*, 85:6002–6.
Chakrabarti, D.K., 1968: The Aryan hypothesis in Indian Archaeology, *Indian Sudies: Past and Present-9(4)*, Calcutta, pp. 343–58.
Chaman Lal, 1978: *India: Cradle of Cultures,* New Delhi. (Ch.I on India and Greece, pp. 300–312)
Chandra, A.N., 1980: *The Rig-Vedic Culture and the Indus Civilisation,* Calcutta (Ch.IX on Indian Conquest of the West, pp. 140–61)
Chapekar, Nalini, M., 1977: *Ancient India and Greece,* Delhi, Ajanta Publications.
Chatterjee, N.C.: *Hindu Politics,* Calcutta.
Chatterjee, S.K., 1962: *Indianism and the Indian Synthesis,* (The Kamala Lectures for the Year 1942) University of Calcutta, Calcutta (Ch. 2 on Indianism: Its Basic Character, pp. 28-52).
Chattopadhyaya, K.P., 1970: *Ancient Indian Cultural Contacts and Migrations,* Calcutta.

Chhabra, B.C. (ed.):1981: *Corpus Inscriptionum Indicarum,* New Delhi.

Childe, V.G., 1915: 'On the date and origin of Minyan ware', *Journal of Hellenic Studies* 35, pp. 196–207.

Childe, V.G., 1926: *The Aryans: A Study of Indo-European Origins,* London, Kegan Paul, Trench & Trubner.

Childe, V.G., 1950: *Prehistoric Migrations in Europe,* Oslo, Aschehoug.

Childe, V.G., 1957: *The Dawn of European Civilization* (6th edn.), London, Routledge & Kegan Paul.

Childe, V.G., 1958: 'Retrospect', *Antiquity* 32, pp. 69–74.

Childe, V.G., 1993: *The Aryans: A Study of Indo-European Origins,* New York, Barnes & Noble.

Choudhary, R.K., 1953: *Studies in Ancient Indian Law and Justice,* Patna, Motilal Banarasidass.

Christopoulos, George, A., 1974: *Prehistory and Protohistory,* Athens, Ekdotike Athenon, S.A.Compan, p. 7.

Clarke, J.J., 1997: *Oriental Enlightenment: the Encounter between Asian and Western Thought,* London, Routledge.

Crossland, R.A., 1971: Immigrants from the North, in I.E.S. Edwards, C.J.Gadd & N.G.L. Hammond (ed.), 1920: *Cambridge Ancient History,* 3rd edn., Cambridge: Cambridge University Press, pp. 824–73, 989–93.

Crossland, Ronald, 1992: 'When specialist collide: archaeology and Indo-European linguistics'—a review of the books of Gamkrelidge & Ivanov; Krntz & Markey and Greppin, In *Antiquity*, 66, No. 250, pp. 251–53.

Cursetji Pavry, J.D.(ed.), 1933: *Studies,* London, Oxford University Press.

Dandekar, R.N., 1972: Universe in Vedic Thought, In *Gonda Congratulatory Volume*, pp. 91–114.

Dandekar, R.N., 1979a: *Insight into Hinduism,* Delhi, Ajanta Publishers.

Dandekar, R.N., 1979b: *Vedic Mythological Tracts,* Delhi, Ajanta Publications, pp. 98, 108, 170–71, 197.

Dani, A. H., 1967: Gandhara Grave Culture, *Ancient Pakistan*-3.

Dani, A. H., 1989: *Perspectives of Pakistan,* Islamabad.

Davar, F.C., 1962: *Iran and India through the Ages,* Bombay, Asia Publishing House.

Davar, F.C., 1970: The Indo-Iranian Age, *Indo-Iranica 23 (1-2)*, pp. 63–69

David Frawley, 1994: *Vedic Aryans and the Origins of Civilization: A Literary and Scientific Perspective,* St. Hyacinthe, Canada.

Dayakrishna, 1996: *The Problematic and Conceptual Structure of Classical Indian Thought about Man, Society and Polity,* Delhi, Oxford University Press.

Deshayes, J., 1960: *Les outils de Bronze L'Indus au Danube,* 2 vols., Paris.

Deshpande, D.Y., 1946: *Ethics of Everyman,* Hind Kitabs, Bombay, Oxford University Press.

Devaraj, N. K., 1988: *Humanism in Indian Thought,* New Delhi.

Devaraj, N. K., 1994: *Hinduism and the Modern Age,* New Delhi.

Devoto G., 1962: *Origin indeuropeo,* Florence, Instituto Italiano di Preistoria e Protoistoria Italiana.

Dhyani, S.N., 1984: *Law-Morality and Justice: Indian Developments,* New Delhi, Metropolitan Book Co. (P) Ltd.

Diakonov, I.M., 1985: On the original home of the speakers of Indo-European, In *Journal of Indo-European Studies, Vol. 13,* pp. 92–174, Washington D.C.

DietzSontheimer, Hermann Kulke, 1997: *Hinduism Reconsidered,* Delhi, Munshiram Manoharlal.

Dixit, S.B., 1969: Bhartiya Jyotish Shastra (Trans. From original Marathi) in Part I of the *History of Astronomy during the Vedic and Vedanga Period,* Manager of Publications, Government of India, Delhi.

Dixitar, V R.R., 1935: *Matsya Puranam—A Study,* Madras, University of Madras.

Dixon, R.M.W., 1992: When specialists collide: archaeology and Indo-European linguistics, a review article in *Antiquity* 66: 251–54.

Dixon, R.M.W., 1997: *The Rise and Fall of Languages,* Cambridge University Press, Cambridge.

Dolgopolsky, Aron B., 1964: "Gipoteza drevnejsego rodstva jazykovyx semi severnoj Eutrasil s verojatnostnoj tochi zrenija", *Voprosy Jazykoznanija* 2:53–63. [English translation In Vitalij V. Shevoroshkin and Thomas L. Markey, eds. *Typology Relationship and Time,* 1986. Ann Arbor, Mich., pp. 27–50].

Dument, P.E. (u.d.) Nelson: 'Indo-Aryan Names from Mitanni, Nuzi and Syrian Documents, *JOBS,* vol. 37.6.

Dutt, N. K., *The Aryanization of India,* Calcutta, K.L. Mukhyopadhyaya.

Edward Craig (Gen.ed.), 1998: *Routledge Encyclopedia of Philosophy,* London.

Edward, Arnold, 1978: *Human Rights,* Eugene Kamcuka, U.S.A.

Erich Fromm, 1947: *Man for Himself,* Greenwich, Conn.

Erman, A., 1907: *Handbook of Egyptian Religion,* (Eng. tr.), London.

Evans, Arhur (Sir), 1921-35: *The Palace of Minos at Knossos,* (4 vols.), London.

Feurestein, George, et al., 1999: *The Search of the Cradle of Civilization,* Delhi, Motilal Banarasidas.

Figulla, H. H., 1963: *Cuneiform Texts from Babylonian Tablets in the British Museum,* London, British Museum.

Finkelberge, M., 1996: "Anatolian languages and Indo-European migrations to Greece", In: *Classical World* 9, pp. 3–20.

Fishkin, James, 1983: *Justice, Equal Opportunity and the Family,* Yale University Press, New Haven.

Flinders Petrie (e.d.): *A History of Egypt,* Vol. II, pp. 262–63.

Floos, Gevin, 1998: *An Introduction to Hinduism,* Cambridge, Cambridge University Press.

Forrer, 1926: *Forschungen,* ii, 1926, pp. 38 ff.

Frankfort, Henri, 1968: *The Birth of Civilization in the Near East,* London, Ernest Benn Limited.

Friedrich, 1929: In *Reallexion der Assyriologie,* I, pp. 144ff.

Freidrich P., 1970: *Proto-Indo-European Trees,* Chicago, Chicago University Press.

Freidrich von Sehlegel, 1849: *The Aesthetics and Miscellaneous Works of Freidrich von Sehlegel*, London, Bohn.

Gadd, C. J., 1932: "Seals of Ancient Indian Style found at Ur", In *Proceedings of the British Academy*- XVIII, London.

Gafurov, B., 1970: Aryans and Indian Civilization, In *Soviet Review,* 7 (35), pp. 8–30.

Gajendragadkar, P.B., 1965: *Law, Liberty and Social Justice,* Asia Publishing House, New Delhi.

Gamkrelidge, T.V. & V.V. Iakonov, 1985a: The Ancient Near East and the Indo-European question: temporal and territorial characteristics of Proto-Indo-European based on linguistics and historico-cultural data, *Journal of Indo-European Studies* 13: 3–48, Washington, D.C.

Gamkrelidge, T.V. & V.V. Iakonov, 1985b: The migration of tribes speaking the Indo-European dialects from their original homeland in the Near East to their historical habitats in Eurasia, *Journal of Indo-European Studies* 13, pp. 49–91, Washington, D.C.

Gamkrelidge, T.V. & V.V. Iakonov, 1985c: The problem of the Original Homeland of the Speakers of the Indo-European languages: in response to I.M. Diakonoff's article, In *Journal of Indo-European Studies* 13: pp. 175ff.

Garstang-Mayer, 1923: *Indes of Hittite names*, and *Liverpool Annals of Archaeology and Anthropology,* x, 1923, pp. 172 ff.

George Sarton, 1959: *Ancient Science and Modern Civilization,* Harper, London.

Ghatage, A. M., 1962: *Historical Linguistics and Indo-Aryan Languages,* Bombay, BUP.

Ghosh, B.K., 1958: The Origin of Indo-Aryan, In *Cultural history of India*, Vol.1, pp. 1–129, Calcutta.

Ghosh, N.N., 1965: Indo-Aryan Literature and Culture: Origins, In *Chaukhambha Sanskrit Studies,* 51, pp. 287 ff.

Ghosh, A., 1989: *Encyclopaedia of Indian Archaeology,* New Delhi, Munshiram Manoharlal.

Gimbutas, M., 1963: 'The Indo-Europeans, archaeological problems', *American Anthropologist* 65, pp. 815–36.

Gimbutas, M., 1970: 'Proto-Indo-European Culture: The Kurgan Culture during the Fifth, Fourth, and Third Millennia BC.' in George Cardona, et al. (eds.): *Indo-European and Indo-Europeans,* 1970, University of Pennsylvania Press, Philadelphia.

Gimbutas, M., 1973: "Old Europe c. 7000-3500 BC: the earliest European civilization before the infiltration of the Indo-European peoples". In: *Journal of Indo-European Studies* 1, pp. 1–21.

Gimbutas, M., 1974: *The Gods and Goddess of Old Europe (7000-3500 BC): Myths, Legends and Cult Images* London, Thames & Hudson.

Gimbutas, M., 1991: *The Language of the Goddess,* San Francisco.

Goetze, A. (u.d.): 'On the Chronology of the Second Millennium B.C.', *Journal of Cuneiform Studies,* Vol. XI, No. 3, p. 63.

Goetze, A, 1928: In *Das Hethiter-Reich* (Der Alte Orient, xxvii, 2, p. 22).

Goetze, Albrecht, 1933: 'Sunassura: An Indian King of Kizwatna', In Cursetji Pavry, pp. 127–29.

Gomperz, T., 1901: *Greek Thinkers,* I (Eng. tr., London).

Gonda J., 1975: *Vedic Literature,* Weisbaden, Germany.

Govind Das, 1908: *Hinduism and India,* London.

Gramkrelidze, T.V. & Ivanov, V.V., 1984: *Indoevropeiski I Indoevropeitsky rekonstruktsiya istoriki-tipologicheskii analiz protokul'tury* (Indo-European and Indo-Europeans: a reconstruction and typological analysis of a proto-language and proto-culture), Tbilisi: Publishing House of the Tbilisi State University.

Greenberg, Joseph H., 1987: *Language in the Americas,* Stanford, Calif.

Gupta, S. P. (ed.), 1995: *The 'Lost' Sarasvati and the Indus Civilization,* Jodhpur, Kusumanjali Prakashan.

Gupta, Sudhir Kumar, 1970: The Aryan Problem, In *Journal of Ganganath Jha Research Institute* 26(1-3), pp. 737–42.

Guslav Kossina, 1902: 'Die Ingogermanische Frage archäologisch uantwortet', *Zeitschrift fur Ethnologie 34,* 161–222 (reprinted in A. Scherer, 1968, *Die Urheimat der indogermanen*, Darmstadt Wissenschaftliche Buchgesellschaft, pp. 25–109.

Gustavo Gutierrez, 1973: *A Theology of Liberation,* New York Orbis Books, Mary Knoll.

Guterbock, Hans G. & Harry A. Hoffner, 1989: *Chicago Hittite Dictionary,* The Oriental Institute of the University of Chicago.

Gyani, S.D., 1961: New Light on the Aryan Problem, in *Proceedings of Indian History Congress,* 24th Session, pp. 31–32.

Gyani, S.D., 1966: Aryan Problem-a new interpretation, in *Proceedings of the Indian History Congress,* 28th Session, pp. 12–22.

Halfass, Wilhem, 1991: *Tradition and Reflection: Explorations in Indian Thought*, Albany.

Hans Jonas, 1963: *The Gnostic Religion,* Boston, Beacon Press.

Hans Kelsen, 1957: *What is Justice?*, University of California Press.

Hardayal, 1970, *The Bodhisattva Doctrine in Buddhist Sanskrit Literature*, Delhi, MBLD, pp. 57–58.

Hariharan, M., 1961: *Hinduism and the Rationalism*, Madras.

Harmatta, J., 1992: On the Emergence of Indo-Iranians: The Indo-Iranian Languages, In A.H.Dani & V. M. Masson (eds.) *History of Civilization in Central Asia,* UNESCO, pp. 357–78.

Harris, A.C., 1992: Kartevelian contacts with Indo-European, in T.L. Markey & J.A.C. Greppin (eds.) *When World Collide:* 37-100, Ann Arbor (MI): Karoma Publishers.

Harvey, David, 1996: *Justice, Nature and Geography of Difference,* Cambridge, Blackwell.

Hastings, James (ed.), 1959: *Encyclopedia of Religion and Ethics,* 12 Volumes, New York.

Hauschild, R., 1962: *Uber die Friihesten Arier imm Alten Orient,* Berlin, p. 62.

Hazra, R.C., 1940: *Studies in the Puranic Records of Hindu Rites and sCustoms,* Dacca.

Hellbom, Anna-Britta, 1963: The Creation Egg, In *Ethnos* 28, pp. 63–105.

Hencken H., 1955: *Indo-European Languages and Archaeology,* (American Anthropologist Memoir 84), New York, American Anthropological Association.

Henze, Carl, 1932: *Mythes et Symboles Lunaires,* Anverse.

Hirsch, Fred, 1977: *Social Limits to Growth,* Routledge & Kegan Paul, London.

Hommel, F., 1898:'Hethiter und Skythen und das erste Augftreten der Iranier in der Geschichte', In *Sitzungsberichte der Bohmischen Akademie, Philologische Klasse,* 1898.

Hood S., 1966: An aspect of the Slav invasions of Greece in the early Byzantine period, *Acta Musei Nationalis Pragae* 20 1(2): 165–71.

Hrozny B., 1931: 'L'entrainement des chevaux chez les anciensindo-europeens d'apres un texte Mitannien-Hittite provenant du mesiecle avant J.C.', *Archiv Orientalni* 3, 431–61.

Hrozny Bedrich, 1953: *Ancient History of Western Asia, India and Crete*, Prague, p. 26.

Hrozny Bedrich, 1959: "The Hittites", In *The Encyclopedia Brittannica,* Vol.11, pp. 598b–608.

Hubert Bonner, 1965: *On Being Mindful of Man,* Boston: Houghton Mifflin Coy.

Illich-Svitych, Vlaislav, 1967: "Materily k sravnitel`nomu slovarju nostraticeskix jazykov", *Etimologija* 1965 (Moscow), 321–73 [English translation in Vitaly Shevoroshkin, ed. *Reconstructing Languages and Cultures,* Bochum, Germany], pp. 125–76.

Ishid Tomoo, 1999: *History and Historical Writing in Ancient Israel,* Leiden, Brill.

Jacobi, Hermann, G., 1894: On the date of the Rigveda (trans. By J. Morrison), In *Indian Antiquary* 23, pp. 154–59.

James, F.T. Bugental, 1965: *The Search for Authenticity,* New York.

James, E.O., 1970: *Creation and Cosmology, A Historical and Comparative Inquiry,* Brill.

James, Gene G. (ed.), 1987: *The Search for Faith in the Twentieth Century,* New York.

Jarrige, J. F., 1975: Excavations at Mehargarh, Pakistan, In *South Asian Archaeology* (ed. J.E.Van Lohinzen de Leeuw), Leiden.

Jarrige, J-F, 1980: The antecedents of civilisation in the Indus Valley, In *Scientific American*-243, no. 2, pp. 122–33.

Jayaswal, K.P., 1955: *Hindu Polity,* Bangalore, pp.184 & 216.

Jolly, Julius, 1975: *Hindu Law and Customs,* Varanasi, Bharatiya Publication House.

Jones, Sir William, 1786: Third Anniversary discourse: 'On the Hindus' Reprinted in the *Collected Works of Sir William Jones* III, 1807, London John Stockdale, pp. 23–46.

Joshi, J. P., (ed.), 1990: *Excavations at Surkotada-1971-72,* New Delhi, Archaeological Survey of India.

Joshi, M. C., 1994: *Hindu Religion and Ethics*, New Delhi. Journal of the Cuneiform Studies, *American School of Oriental Studies (JAOS).*

Kammenhuber, A., 1961: *Hippologia Heathica,* Weisbaden, pp. 15–21.

Kammenhuber, A., 1969: 'Das Hattische', in Spuler (ed.): 428–546, 584–8.

Kant, Immanuel, 1934: *Religion within the Limits of Reason Alone,* trans. Greene, T. M. and Hudson, H. H, The Open Court Publishing Company, Chicago.

Kant, Immanuel, 1965: *The Metaphysical Elements of Justice,* trans. By Ladd, John, Indiana University Press, Indianapolis.

King, Leonard W, 1915: *A History of Babylon,* London, Chatto & Windus.

Kinnier, Wilson, J.V., 1974: *Indo-Sumerian,* Oxford.

Knapp, Bernard Bernark, 1991: *The History and Culture of Ancient Western Asia and Egypt,* New York, Wadsworth Publishing Company.

Kohl, P.L., 1978: "The Western Asian Trade in the Third Millennium BC", In *Current Archaeology,* 19, pp. 463–92.

Kohl, P.L., 1979: "The 'world-economy' of West Asia in the Third Millennium BC." In M. Taddei (ed.): *South Asian Archaeology,* 1977, Naples, pp. 55–85.

Krammer, Samuel Noah, 1961: *History begins at Summer,* London, Thames & Hudson.

Kramrisch, Stella, 1962-63, The Triple Structure of Creation in the RigVeda, In *History of Religion* 2, pp. 140–47; 256–85.

Krantz, Grover S., 1988: *Geographical Development of European Languages,* New York, Peter Lang Publishing.

Kuiper, F.B.J., 1970, Cosmogony and Conception: a query, In *History of Religion* 10(2), pp. 91–138.

Lal, B.B., 1997: *The Earliest Civilization of South Asia,* Delhi, Books & Books.

Lal, B.B., 2002: *The Sarasvati Flows On: The Continuity of Indian Culture,* New Delhi, Aryan Books International.

Lamont, Corliss, 1965: *The Philosophy of Humanism,* New York, Frederick Ungan Publishing Company..

Lamperis, Timothy, J., 1984: *Hindu Influence on Greek Philosophy: The Odyssey of the Soul from the Upanishads to Plato,* Calcutta, Minerva Associates.

Lamperis, Timothy, J., 1994: *Hinduism and the Modern Age,* New Delhi.

Laurie L. Patton (ed.), 1994: *Authority, Anxiety, and Cannon: Essays in Vedic Interpretation,* Albany, State University of New York Press.

Leonard, W. King, 1915: *A History of Babylon,* London, Chatts & Windus.

Lincoln, Bruse, 1975: The Indo-European Myth of Creation, In *History of Religions,* 15, pp. 121–145.

Luckenbill, D.D., 1921: In *American Journal of Semitic Languages,* xxxvii, 1921, pp. 180 ff.

Macdonell, A. A. & Keith, A.B, 1967: *Vedic Index* (2 vols.), (Reprint) N. Delhi, Motilal Banarasidas (originally published from London in 1912).

Macintyre, Alasdair, 1988: *Whose Justice? Which Rationality?,* Duckworth, London.

Mackay, F. J. H., 1925: "Sumerian Contacts with Ancient India." In

Journal of the Royal Asiatic Society of Great Britain and Ireland, pp. 679–701.

Mahony, Williamk, 1998: *The Artful Universe: An Introduction to the Vedic Religious Imagination,* Albany: State University of New York Press.

Mainkar, V. B., 1984: Metrology in the Indus Civilization, In Lal, B.B. & S. P. Gupta, 1984, *Frontiers of the Indus Civilization*, pp. 141–152.

Majumdar, R.C., 1948: Indian Culture as a Factor in World Civilization. In *Sir William Jones Centenary Volume,* Calcutta.

Mallory, J.P., 1989: *In Search of the Indo-Europeans,* London.

Mallory J.P., 1991: *In Search of the Indo-Europeans: Language, Archaeology and Myth,* New York, Thames & Hudson.

Mallory J.P., & Adams D.Q. (eds.), 1997: *Encyclopedia of Indo-European Culture,* London, Fitzroy Dearborn.

Mallowan, M.E.L., 1965: *Early Mesopotamia and Iran,* London.

Margaret Knight, 1961: *Humanist Anthology: From Confucius to Bertrand Russel,* Barry & Rockliff, London.

Markey T.L. & Greppin, John A., 1990: *When Worlds Collide: Indo-Europeans and Pre-Indo-Europeans. The Bellagria Papers* (Linguistica Extranea, Studia 19), Ann Arbor, MI: Karona Publishers.

Mashak, A., 1972: *The Cognitive Beginning of Man's First Art*, New York.

Masson, V. M. & Sarianidi, V.I., 1972: *Central Asia: Turkmenia Before the Achaemenids,* London.

Matthew Arnold, 1875: *Culture and Anarchy,* London.

Mercer, A. B. (ed.), 1982: 'Tussratta's Letters to Amenophis 11, nos. 22, 25, 26', In *The Tell el-Amarna Tablets,* Vol. 1, Toronto.

Meyer, C., (ed.) 1908: In *Zeitschrift fur vergleichende Sprachforschung,* xlii, 1908, 16 ff.

Meyer, C. (ed.) 1928: *Geschichte des Altertums,* ii. 1, 1928, p. 158, note 1.

Mill J.S., 1969: *Collected Works*, University of Toronto Press.

Miller, David, 1976: *Social Justice*, Clarendon Press.

Miller, Jeanine, 1985: *The Vision of the Cosmic Order in the Vedas,* London, Routledge & Kegan Paul.

Mircea Eliade, 1984: Cosmogonic Myth and Sacred History, In Alan Dunde's *Sacred Narrative,* Berkeley.

Mircea Eliade, 1987: *The Encyclopedia of Religion,* Vol. 16, New York, Macmillan Publishing Company.

Misra, S.S., 1969: *A Comparative Grammar of Sanskrit, Greek and Hittite,* Calcutta, The World Press.

Misra, S.S., 1980: *Fresh Light on Indo-European Classification & Chronology*, Varanasi, Ashutosh Prakashan Sansthan.

Misra, Janardan, 1988: *Veda and Bharat, India*, New Delhi, S.S. Publishing.

Misra, S.S., 1992: *The Aryan Problem: A Linguistic Approach*, New Delhi, Munshi Manohar Lal Publishers Pvt. Ltd.

Misra, V. N., 1994: Indus Civilization and the Rigvedic Sarasvati, In *South Asian Archaeology, 1993, II, Helsinki*, pp. 511–25

Mitra, Rajendra Lal, 1969: *Indo Aryans: Contributions towards the Elucidation of their Ancient and Mediaeval history*, (2 Vols.), Delhi, Indological Book House.

Modi, J.J., 1932: *Oriental Conference Papers*, Bombay, Fort Printing Press.

Moscati, Sabatino, 1963: *The Face of the Ancient Orient*, London, Routledge & Kegan Paul.

Mukherjee, R.K., 1942: *Ashoka*, Delhi.

Murty, S.R.N., 1997: *Vedic View: A Geological Insight into the Vedas*, New Delhi, D.K. Printworld.

Nag, Kalidas, 1954: *India and the Middle East*, Calcutta, M.C.Sarkar & Sons Ltd.

Nancy Thomson De-Grummond (ed.), 1996: *An Encyclopedia of the History of Classical Archaeology*, Wesport: Greenwood Press.

Nehru, Jawaharlal, 1972: *Selected Works of Jawaharlal Nehru*, Vol. III, Orient Longman.

Nelson, J. H., 1981: *The Scientific Study of Hindu Law*, London, Kegan Paul.

Ojibenin, B.L., 1968: *The Structure of the Mythological Texts of the RigVeda: The Vedic Cosmogony* (In Russian), Nauka, Moscow.

Olmstead, A.T., 1951: *History of Assyria*, Chicago, Chicago University Press.

Oppenheim A. Leo, 1988: "The Seafaring Merchants of Ur', In *Journal of American Oriental Society*, 74, pp. 6–17.

Orians, R.B., 1998: *The Origins of European Thought about the Body, the Mind, the Soul, the World, Time and Fate*, Cambridge University Press, Cambridge.

Orieux, Claude, 1999: *A History of Ancient Greece*, Massachusetts, Blackwell Publishing.

Panagi, Narayan Bhawan Rao, 2001: *The Vedic Fathers of Geology*, New Delhi, Cosmo Publishing.

Pande, R.B., 1957: *Indian Palaeography*, Varanasi, Motilal Banarasidas.

Pande, G.C., 1984: *Foundations of Indian Culture*, N. Delhi, Books & Books (2 vols.).

Pande, G.C.(ed.), 1999: *The Dawn of Indian Civilization (up to c. 600 BC)*, Vol. 1 Part 1 of the History of Science, Philosophy and Culture in Indian Civilization, Delhi, PHISPC.

Pande, G.C., 1992: *The Cosmogonic Legends of the Brahmanas*, Gorakhpur.

Pande, G.C., 2001: *Vaidika Sanskriti* (in Hindi), Allahabad, Loka Bharati.

Pandit, Nanak Chanda, 1951: *The Wisdom of India*, New Delhi.

Panikkar, K. M., 1964: *Hinduism and the West*, Chandigarh.

Pargiter, F.E., 1962: *Ancient Indian Historical Tradition*, (Reprint) Delhi, Motilal Banarasidas.

Pearson, J.D., 1966: *Oriental and Asian Bibliography: An Introduction with Some Reference to Africa*, Bombay, V.D. Willis.

Penner, Hans H., 1966: Cosmogony as Myth in the Vishnu Purana, In *History of Religions*, 5, pp. 283–99.

Peter Laslett & W.G. Runciman (eds.), 1964: *Philosophy, Politics and Society*, Basil Blackwell.

Petrie, Flinders, 1923: *A History of Egypt* (3 vols.), see Xth edition, London, vol. 2, pp. 262–63.

Phillip Berryman, 1987: *Liberation Theology*, Pantheon Books, New York.

Picket A., 1877: *Les origines Indo-Europeans*, Paris, Sandoz et Fischbaker.

Porzig, 1927: *Zeitschrift fur Indologie und Iranistik*, V, p. 267.

Possehl, Gregory, L., 1999: *Indus Age: The Beginnings*, Philadelphia, University of Pennsylvania Press.

Prasad, Amba, 1970: 'India's Contacts with Africa from the Earliest times', In *Vivekananda Committee*, 1970, pp. 601–13.

Prichard, James B., (u.d.): *Ancient Near Eastern Texts*, pp. 241–45.

Rajaram N.S, 1993: *Aryan Invasions of India: The Myth and the Truth*, New Delhi.

Rajaram N.S. & David Frawley, 1994: *Vedic Aryans and the Origins of Civilization: A Literary and Scientific Perspective*, St. Hacinthe, Canada.

Ramat, Anna Giacalone & Paolo Ramat (eds.), 1998: *The Indo-European Languages*, London, Routledge.

Rambhachan, Anatanand, 1991: *Accomplishing the Accomplished: the Vedas as a Source of Valid Knowledge in Samkara*, Honolulu, University of Hawaii Press.

Rangacharya, M., 1957: *The Hindu Philosophy of Conduct*, Calcutta.

Rao, S.R., 1961: Lothal and West Asia, In the monograph of the *Archaelogical Survey of India*, 1961, pp. 44–46.

Rao, S.R., 1991: *Dawn and Devolution of Indus Civilization*, New Delhi, Aditya Prakashan.

Rawlinson, H. G., 1977: *Intercourse Between India and the Western World (From the Earliest Times to the Fall of Rome)*, (Reprint), Delhi, Rai Book Service.

Rawls, John, 1958: Justice as Fairness, in *Philosophical Review* 67.

Rawls, John, 1964: Justice As Fairness, In Laslett Peter & W.G. Runciman (eds.), *Philosophy, Politics and Society*, Basil Blackwell.

Rawls, John, 2001: *Justice as Fairness: A Restatement*, Cambridge, Harvard University Press.

Raychoudhuri, H. C., 1958: *Studies in Indian Antiquities*, 2nd Edition, University of Calcutta, Calcutta.

Renfrew, Lord Colin, 1987: *Archaeology and Language: The Puzzle of Indo-European Origins*, Cambridge University Press, New York.

Renfrew C., 1988: Review of C. Renfrew, 1987: Author's precis in *Current Anthropology* 29:437–41.

Renfrew, Colin, 2000: 'At the Edge of Knowability: Towards a prehistory of Languages', In *Cambridge Archaeological Journal* 10:1.

Rollo May, 1970: *Motivation and Personality* (2nd edn.), New York.

Roy, Ramashraya, 1999: *Beyond Ego's Domain: Being and Order in The Vedas*, Delhi, Shipra Publications.

Roy, Ramashraya, 2000: *Aspects of Social Justice in India*, A key note address in the National Seminar of M.P.I.S.S.R, Ujjain.

Ruhlen, Meritt, 1994: *On the Origin of Languages: Studies in Linguistic Taxonomy*, Stanford University Press, California.

Said, Edward W., 1985: *Orientalism*, Harmondsworth (Penguin).

Saiyidain, K.G., 1966: *Humanist Tradition in Indian Educational Thought*, London.

Sankaranand, 1962: *Hindu States of Sumeria: When India Ruled the West*, Calcutta.

Sardar, Ziauddin, 1999: *Orientalism*, Buckingham, Open University Press.

Sayce, A.H., 1933: Indians in Western Asia in the Fifteenth Century B.C., In *Cursetji Pavry*, 1933, pp. 399–402.

Schapiro, 1966: *The Emergence of Liberal Humanism*, New York: McGraw-Hill Book.

Scheftelowitz, 1902: In *Zeitschrift fur vergleichende Sprachforschung, xxxviii*, 1902, p. 270 ff.

Schliemann, H., 1878: *Mycenae*, Leipzig.

Schliemann, H., 1880a: *A Narrative of Researches and Discoveries at Mycenae and Tiryns*, New York.

Schliemann, H., 1880b: *Ilios the City and Country of Trojans*, London.

Schrader, O., 1972: *Prehistoric Antiquities of the Aryan People*, (Reprint) Delhi, Oriental Publishers (originally published in 1890, New York).

Schweitzer, Albert, 1951: *Indian Thought and Its Development,* trans. C.E.B. Russel, Adam and Charles Black, London.

Sebeok, Thomas A. (ed.), 1964: *Style in Language*, Cambridge: MIT Press.

Sebeok, Thomas A. (ed.), 1966: *Portraits of Linguistics* I, Bloomington (IN), Indiana University Press.

Sedlar, Jean W., 1980: *India and the Greek World*, New Jersey, Rowman and Littlefield Totowa.

Sehgal, Sunil, 1999: *Encyclopedia of Hinduism,* New Delhi, Sarup & Sons.

Sen, A. K., 1926: *Hindu Political Thought,* Delhi.

Sen, Sukumar, 1958: *History and Pre-History of Sanskrit*, University of Mysore Extension Lectures, Mysore.

Senn, Alfred, et al. (eds.), 1970: *Indo-European and Indo-Indo-Europeans,* University of Pennsylvania Press, Philadelphia.

Sethna, K.D., 1992: *The Problem of Aryan Origins: From Indian Point of View*, New Delhi, Aditya Prakashan.

Sethna, K.D., 1997: *Ancient India in a New Light,* New Delhi, Aditya Prakashan.

Shaffer, Jim G.: 1984: The Indo-Aryan Invasions: Cultural Myth and Archaeological Reality, In John R. Lucas (ed.) *The People of South Asia: The Biological Anthropology of India, Pakistan and Nepal,* New York, pp. 77–90.

Shamashastri, R.R. (trans.), 1960: *Arthashastra,* 6th Edition, Mysore.

Shanks, Michael, 1997: *Classical Archaeology of Greece: Experiences of the Discipline,* London, Routledge.

Sharma, D.S., 1961: *Hinduism through the Ages,* Bombay.

Sharma, S.D., 1988: *Administration of Justice in Ancient India*, New Delhi, Harman Publishing House.

Sharma Ramvilas, 1994: *Paschimi Asia aur Rigveda,* Delhi.

Shashtri, Motilal, 1950: *History of Indian Cosmogonical Ideas,* New Delhi, Munshiram Manoharlal.

Shastri, K.N., 1961: New Light on the Indus Civilization and early contact with Iraq and Iran, In the monograph of the *Archaelogical Survey of India*, 1961, pp. 51–53.

Sherrat, A & S, 1988: The Archaeology of Indo-European: An Alternative View, In *Antiquity-62,* pp. 584–95.

Shivesh Thakur & Ninian Swart (eds.), 1993: *Ethical and Political Dilemmas of Modern India,* London, Macmillan.

Singh, Bhagawan, 1995: *Vedic Harappans,* New Delhi, Aditya Prakashan.

Singh, Jaideep, 1979: *The Humanistic View of Man,* IIPA, New Delhi.

Singh, Ram Charit, 1959 & 1961: Homeland of the Aryans, in the *Journal of the Bihar Research Society*, nos. 45(1-4), pp. 498–505; 47(1-4), pp. 290–311 respectively.

Singhal, D.P., 1972: *India and World Civilization,* (2 vols.) Delhi, Rupa & Co.

Sircar, D.C., 1983: *Select Inscriptions*, Delhi, Motilal Banarasidas.

Sivaswamy Aiyer, P.S., 1986: *Evolution of Hindu Moral Ideas*, New Delhi.

Smith, V. A., 1889: Graeco-Roman Influence on the Civilization of Ancient India, In, *Journal of Royal Asiatic Society,* London.

Spesier, E.A., 1924: A Letter of Shanshshater and the Date of the Kirkuk Tablets, In *Journal of American Oriental Society,* Vol. 49, pp. 269–75.

Speziale, Arturo, 1987: *Ethical and Religious Value of Ancient India: 3000 BC- 650 AD,* Calcutta, Sujan Pub.

Srejovic, D., 1972: *Europe's First Monumental Sculptures, New Discoveries at Lepinsky Vir,* London.

Steffani, Ruggero, 1964: 'KUB XXI C 33 (BO487): Musilis', In *Journal of American Oriental Society,* Vol. 84, pp. 22–30.

Stephen, Shute & Susan Hurley (eds.), 1993: *On Human Rights: The Oxford Amnesty Thought about Man, Society and Polity,* Oxford University Press, Delhi.

Stutley, Margaret and James, 1977: *A Dictionary of Hinduism,* New Delhi, Allied Publishers.

Surya Kant, 1981: A Practical Vedic Dictionary, Delhi, Oxford University Press.

Swami Vivekananda, 1947: *Caste Culture and Socialism.*

Taulor, Isaac, 1892: *The Origin of the Aryans*, 2nd edn., London, Walter Scott.

Thakur, Shivesh C., 1996: *Religion and Social Justice*, Macmilan Press Ltd., London.

Thapar, B. K., 1970: The Aryans: a reappraisal of the Problem, in *Vivekanand Commemoration Volume,* Madra, pp. 147–64.

Thieme, Paul, 1960: The 'Aryan' Gods of the Mitanni Treaties, In *Journal of the American Oriental Society* 80(4), pp. 301–17.

Tilak, Balgangadhar, 1904 (1894): *The Orion or Researches in the Antiquity of the Vedas,* Bombay.

Toporov, V.N., 1967: About the Reconstruction of the World-egg myth, In *UZ TUS,* VYP, 198, pp. 81–99.

Tripathi, D.N., 1988: *Archaeology and Tradition,* New Delhi, Ramanand Vidya Bhawan.

Tripathi, D.N., 2000: 'New Archaeology and Vedic Cosmogony', In *Man and Environment*, Vol. XXV (1), pp. 1–17, Pune.

Tull, H. W., 1992: *The Vedic Origins of Karma: Cosmos as Man in Ancient Indian Myth and Ritual,* Albany, NY: SUNY Press.

Unger, 1926: 'Kiswatna' in *Rellexikon der Virgeschichte,* vi, 1926, p. 366 ff.

Verma, Vishnu Kant, 2001: *Indo-Aryan Colonization of Greece and Middle East,* 2 vols., Delhi, Pratibha Prakashan.

Vivekananda Committee, 1970: *India's Contribution to World Thought and Culture,* Vivekananda Rock Memorial Committee, Madras.

Waddell, L. A., 1968: *The Makers of Civilization in Race & History,* (Reprint) Delhi, S. Chand.

Ward, Donald J., 1970: An Indo-European Mythological themes in Germanic Tradition." In *Indo-European and Indo-Europeans,* Philadelphia, pp. 405–20.

Weidner, 1923: In *Zeitschrift für Indologie und Iranistik,* V, 1927, pp. 88ff.

Wheeler, R.E.M., 1968: *The Indus Civilisation,* (3rd edn.) Cambridge, Supplementary Volume to the Cambridge History of India.

Winternitz, H., 1972: *History of Indian Literature, 2 Vols*, New Delhi, Oriental Books (Reprint).

Woodcock, George, 1966: *The Greeks in India,* London, Faber & Faber.

Woolley, Leonard (Sir), 1927: *The Royal Cemetery, Ur Excavations* (2 vols.), London.

Woolley, Leonard (Sir), 1955: *Excavations at Ur,* London, Ernest Benn.

Yadava, B.R., 1987: *Vedic Cosmogony,* Aligarh, Vigyan Prakashan.

Ziauddin, Sardar, 1999: *Orientalism,* Buckingham, Open University Press.

Index